eBay® SCAMS!

PROTECT YOURSELF AS YOU MASTER eBay®

MARK GABRIEL

Illustrations by Matthew Brady

eBay® Scams – Protect Yourself As You Master eBay®

info@mimosabooks.com

ISBN 0-9735328-3-1

Printed in the United States of America.

Dedicated to all the scammers out there.

Your days are numbered.

About the Author

"Hanging around with the wrong kind of people" That's the answer Mark Gabriel gave us when we asked him how he knew so much about the scammers on eBay. Mark Gabriel has been using eBay since the early days and has written and developed several learning pieces on the topic. His goal has always been to stamp out scammers, one scam at a time. With this book, he's even closer to meeting that goal.

Mark has developed extensive amounts of curriculum and learning tools across a wide range of technical and non-technical topics. Mark has recently worked on several books with topics covering: music editors, image editing software, auction sites and hardware.

Acknowledgments

This book would not have been possible without the support of the following people:

- My wife. You're an angel. You continue to make me the happiest man in the world.
- My daughter. You are the daughter of an angel and I thank God for you everyday.
- My parents. Your unconditional love and support over the years is inspirational.
- Andrew L. Smith. Thank you for allowing us to use your film Reawakening in our book. Visit www.nilsix.com.
- Scammers worldwide. Without all of you, this book wouldn't of been possible.

Hopefully one day, this book won't be necessary.

Preface

Nobody ever wants to gets ripped off.

I was at a party recently where I came upon a small group having a discussion about eBay. Curious, I inched myself closer so I could eavesdrop into their conversation. I overheard the following comments being made:

- Is eBay actually safe?
- I heard that Rob got scammed out of $5000!
- How do I know the seller is really going to send me my stuff once I've paid?
- I read in the paper that some kid stole thousands of dollars from eBay buyers!

I took the opportunity to introduce myself and began asking them questions. One hour later, as my wife looked at her watch, I was still wrapped up with these people discussing this online auction house phenomenon.

Once the party ended and the smoke had cleared - it hit me. These people had never really experienced eBay themselves but rather had friends who had been scammed, heard about someone being scammed or just feared being scammed. The operative word in this statement is “fear”. Bottom line - fear of the unknown.

The concept for this book was born that day.

There are, what seems like hundreds of eBay books out there that spend a lot of time on how to search, buy, sell, etc. None I could find that actually focused on informing and educating readers about existing scams or how to protect and defend themselves.

My research has shown that there are three types of people out there:

1) Those who have been scammed and…

2) Those who are paralyzed with fear of being scammed and…

3) Those who know someone who has been scammed

This book is for all of you.

eBay is not a scary place. In fact, eBay is an incredibly safe place where they claim that less than one-one-hundredth of 1 percent of all listings are fraudulent. This is an extremely low percentage. There is a lot of hype around scamming and it really has people running scared.

Further to this statistic, many people have no idea how hard eBay works to ensure their online system is scam and fraud free. They’ve put together taskforces, developed software systems, provided toolbar downloads and they consistently collaborate with all law enforcement agencies. It is their number one priority to keep all of you safe and they are doing an incredible job considering the staggering number of people on their site each day.

For any of you scammers who may have picked up this book – we're on to you. Don't even think of using this book for evil. By the time you wipe the scum from your eyes, everyone will already be wise to these scams and they just won't work.

Remember - knowledge is power. My primary goal is to make all of you aware of the various scams taking place throughout eBay.com and other online auctions. Think defense and prevention. This book will give you the confidence you need to comfortably and securely buy and sell on eBay.

The Contents Explained

This book is broken up into three distinct parts: The eBay Way, The Scamming Scammers and the Scams they Play, and the Appendices.

Part 1: The eBay Way

Here, we cover off the basics and ensure you have a strong overview knowledge of eBay and how it works. This includes eBay's beginnings, registering, searching, bidding, buying and selling. With these basics under your belt, you will be ready jump right in and do some buying and selling – with confidence!

Part 2: The Scamming Scammers and the Scams they Play

Yecch. This is the icky part. Here, we cover off all the scams that have reared their ugly heads at some point on either eBay or other online auction sites. In the unlikely event that one is pointed in your direction – you'll be ready. You'll be ready to fight, defend or stand hard depending on the strategy you choose. Join me as I disect these scams and list the different ways they can be prevented.

Part 3: Appendices

I created two Scam-Aids that I think will really come in handy as you buy and sell on eBay. Set up as checklists, these two Scam-Aids should never leave your computer's side. They serve as excellent reminders and quick access to many of the valuable tips provided in this book. There is also an appendix that covers the scams that didn't quite make it into the book as full blown scams.

Remember – there is nothing to fear but fear itself. eBay is an extremely safe place but it's important to be smart and informed. Good luck out there and may your eBay transactions always remain scam-free.

Table of Contents

PART I The eBay Way

Chapter 1 Welcome to the eBay Way

Chapter 2 Moving Along the eBay Way

Chapter 3 Help is on the Way

Chapter 4 The Art of the Search

Chapter 5 Bidding and Buying

Chapter 6 Time to Sell

Chapter 7 My Very Own eBay

PART II The Scams

Chapter 8 Gold Plated Shipping

Chapter 9 Misleading Titles & Descriptions

Chapter 10 Shilling

Chapter 11 Phishing

Chapter 12 Pyramid Scams

Chapter 13 Sniping

Chapter 14 Defect Reject Scam

Chapter 15 Spamming

Chapter 16 Second Chance Scam

Chapter 17 Phantom Bidding

Chapter 18 Feedback Padding Scam

Chapter 19 The Photo Doctor

Chapter 20 Win a Car Scam

Chapter 21 The Shield Scam

Chapter 22 Electronics for Free Scam

Chapter 23 MIA Scam

Chapter 24 Dictionary Attacks

Chapter 25 Check the Big Checks

Chapter 26 Help Wanted Scam

Chapter 27 Grow your Own Escrow

Chapter 28 Fire Sale Scam

PART III Appendices

Appendix A - Checklists

Appendix B - Scam Bites

eBay Scams Presents

THE ADVENTURES OF

SCAMMAN

CHAPTER 1

Welcome to the eBay Way

Welcome to the eBay Way

For many of you, this may be your first experience using eBay, so I think formal introductions are not only polite, but required. In this chapter, we will cover:

- How did it all begin?
- What can you buy and sell on eBay?
- Are there other auction sites out there?

How Did It All Begin?

eBay was first introduced way back in 1995 by a man named Pierre Omidyar and his girlfriend at the time (now his wife). The two originally had one goal in mind – trading Pez candy dispensers using the world wide web – a.k.a. – the Internet. Originally, this online site was called AuctionWeb but was later renamed after the site's domain name *ebay.com*.

If you're wondering how Omidyar came up with the name eBay, you may be surprised to hear that it wasn't his first choice. Omidyar had formed a sole proprietorship for his consulting business and named it Echo Bay Technology Group. Why Echo Bay you ask? According to Omidyar, "It just sounded cool". The next logical step was to register the name EchoBay.com and continue along his merry way. Unfortunately, when he tried, he discovered that he was too late. A company out of Canada called Echo Bay Mines had beaten him to the punch and snatched up the domain name he wanted. Taking what he thought was the next best thing, Omidyar registered what has become one of the most popular sites on the Internet: eBay.com.

Although, in its beginnings, the service eBay provided to its members was free, they soon started charging in order to cover their ISP costs.

Nine years later, tens of millions of people buy and sell on eBay daily - turning this site into one of the Internet's most successful businesses.

Feel more at ease now? Well, with those formal introductions now behind us, let's get a better idea of how this online monster works.

What Can You Buy and Sell on eBay?

I always have a lot of fun when it comes to this question. If you are new to eBay, you may be surprised at the sheer number of items for sale on eBay. You'll be even more surprised when you see the kinds of items that are up for sale on eBay. When people ask me this question, my answer is always the same: pretty much anything. Think of eBay as the world's largest garage sale. Forget your local yard sales, flea markets and bazaars - there's another venue in town and he's bigger, got more to choose from and you don't have to change out of your pajamas or leave your home in order to participate.

Do you have anything to sell on eBay? You better believe you do. After one spring cleaning, I found a wealth of items to sell. Everything from my old coin collection to my He-Man figures were potential goldmines on eBay. Take it one step further and do what a good friend of mine did. He offered his friends and families a service. He would clean their homes, garages, basements if he was allowed to keep any of the junk they deemed worthless. You'd be surprised at the number of items he's sold on eBay using this technique. The old adage, "one man's trash is another man's treasure" couldn't be more true than in this example.

There are so many strange and wonderful things to sell and buy on eBay that it would take a whole book to list them. Let's take a look at some examples of items that are either currently or have recently been sold on eBay. I think this list may even surprise the most veteran of eBayers out there.

Truth or Scam?

The real question here is: Truth or Scam? You're going to see items listed here that are going to be really hard to believe. Many of these sellers may actually have a real, tangible item for sale. They may believe that what they are selling is genuine. That's what makes the whole idea of policing (on eBay's end) very difficult. Take a look at some of those items that in my opinion straddle the line between truth and scam. Ultimately, you, the eBay buyer will have to be the judge – keeping that famous saying "Caveat Emptor" firmly tucked in the back of your mind!

Matches used by Mick Jagger

Imagine – someone picking up matches that Mick Jagger used and selling them on eBay? Believe it or not – stranger things have happened. In my humble opinion, this one probably doesn't come with a certificate of authenticity. (See Figure 1.1)

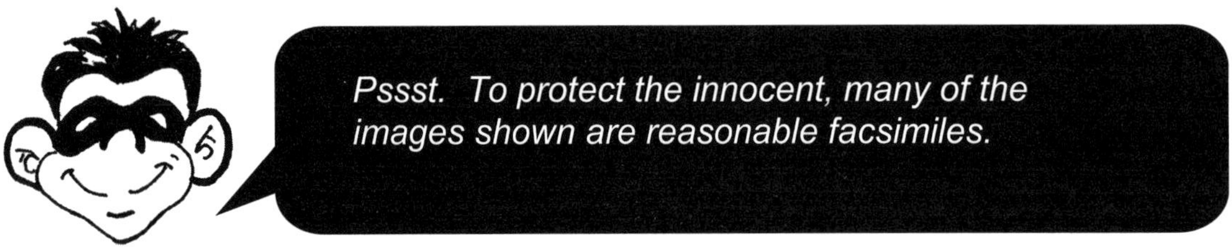

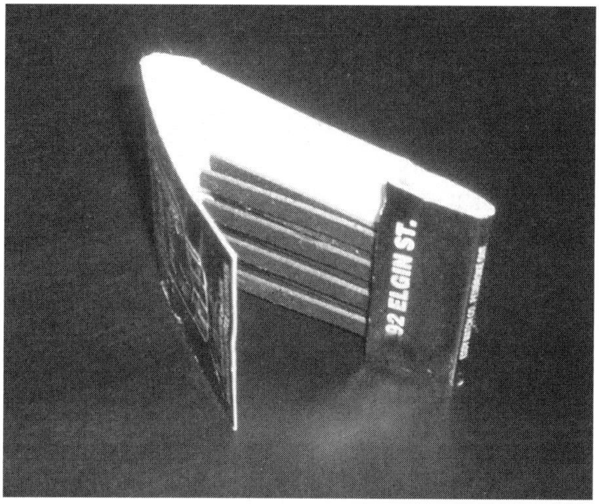

Figure 1.1 Matches used by Mick Jagger

Ghost in a Bottle

Spooky stuff! This bottle not only contains a ghost but it also brings the owner plenty of bad luck – so be careful on this one. Serious bidders only. (See Figure 1.2)

Figure 1.2 Spooky ghost in a bottle

Rare, unappraised gems, get rich?

Notice the question mark in that title? The winning bidder will get themselves a bag full of rare and exotic gems found in a mine somewhere north of Manitoba. (See Figure 1.3)

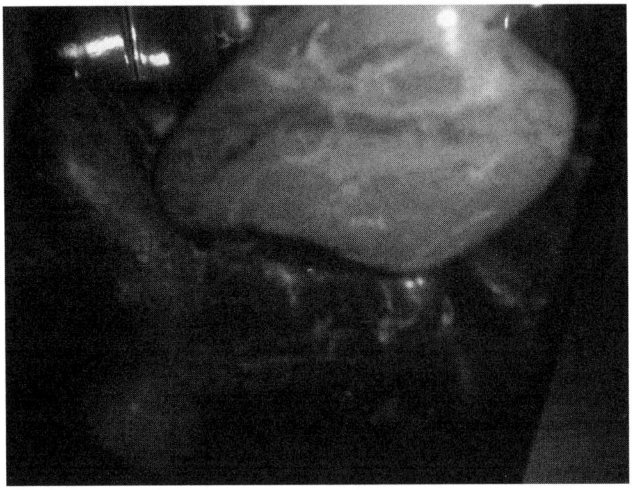

Figure 1.3 Rare gems for sale

Absolutely Nothing

Believe it or not, this was a popular sale item on eBay. Personally, this looks like a feedback purchase scam but who am I to judge? More on that scam in a later chapter. (See Figure 1.4)

Newlywed For Hire

For a low opening bid price of $9.99, you can win the chance to spend some time with this hunky newlywed. Do we have any bidders? (See Figure 1.5)

Figure 1.4 Buy yourself absolutely nothing!

Figure 1.5 Buy a date with this hunk

Liberace's Last Will & Testament

Were you a fan? Get your hands on this hot item and complete your collection. (See Figure 1.6)

Figure 1.6 Liberace's last will

Advertise on my Body

What this member is selling is actual advertising space on her body. If you win, simply send her what you want printed and she will paint it on her body (your choice of location) for a specified period of time. The higher your bid amount, the longer she sports the ad. Again, this may be tough one to police – especially if she's in a different country from you. (See Figure 1.7)

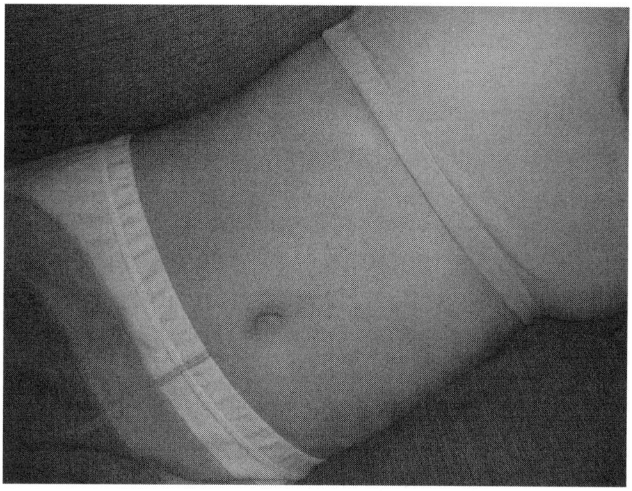

Figure 1.7 Excellent piece of ad real estate

Used Tom Cruise Tissues

Why wouldn't you bid on this item? Die-hard Cruise fans will surely line up for an item like this. DVD in image is not included. (See Figure 1.8)

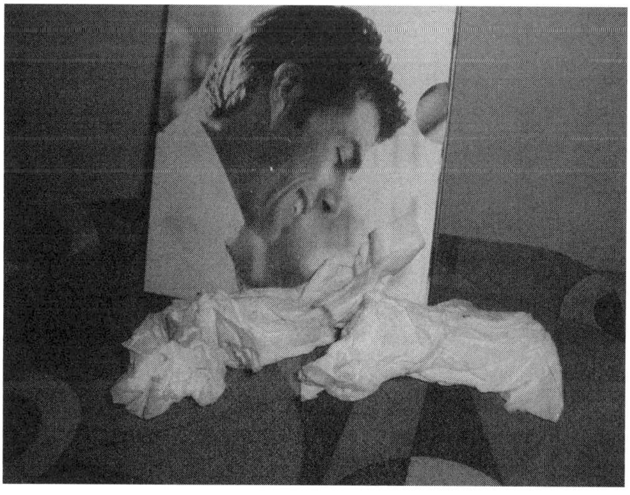

Figure 1.8 Used tissues from Tom Cruise

Freaky Diet Pill - Lose Weight Magically

Pop this pill and the weight will simply fall off, claims this listing. Good luck everyone! (See Figure 1.9)

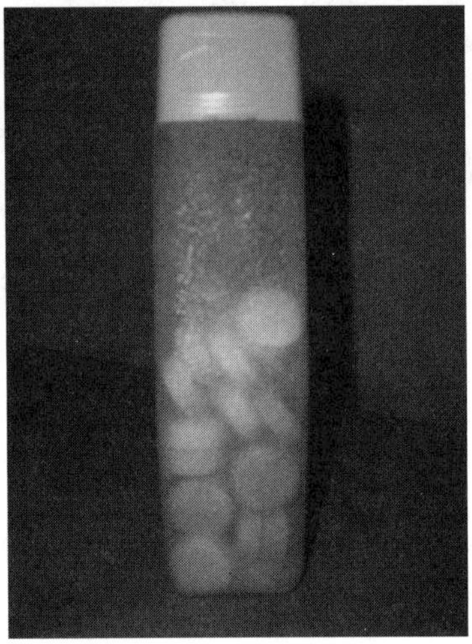

Figure 1.9 Lose weight with these pills

Live Forever Magic Ring

Wear this ring for 1 year straight without ever removing it and this winning bidder will live forever. Would you believe this image was not photo edited? (See Figure 1.10)

Magic Hand Cloth

Like magic, anything you wipe with this hand cloth will fade away. Use it on sofa stains, clothing stains, wrinkles, blackheads and scars. (See Figure 1.11)

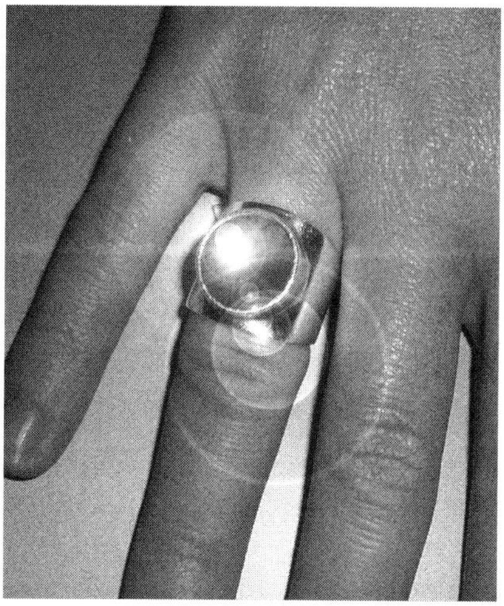

Figure 1.10 Live forever wearing this ring.

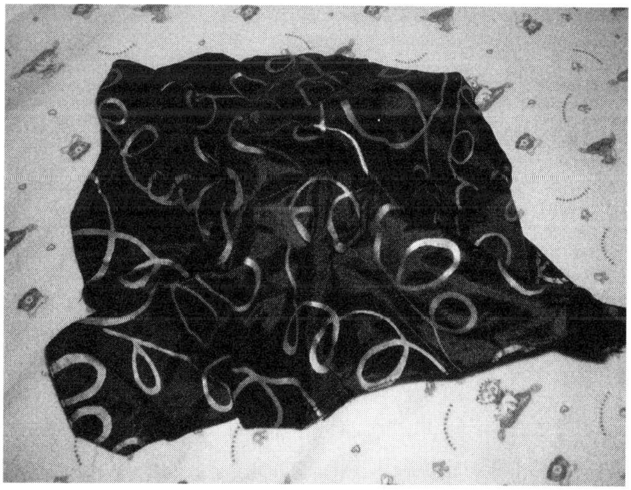

Figure 1.11 Instant stain, blemish, wrinkle and scar remover

Instant Hypnotizer

Meet people of the opposite sex a whole lot easier by hypnotizing them first. Sway this ancient pendant in front of your potential partner's eyes and watch the magic as they fall instantly in love with you. (See Figure 1.12)

Figure 1.12 Hypnotize your partners and get true love

Win a 1 hour Conversation with Me

That's right! Check me out in that picture. That's who you'll be talking to if you win this auction – for one whole hour! (See Figure 1.13)

Figure 1.13 Win a one hour conversation with her!

Witch Craft Ink Bat Blood

Tired of traditional pens that constantly run out of ink? Pump this pen full of bat blood white ink and you'll never have that problem again. (See Figure 1.14)

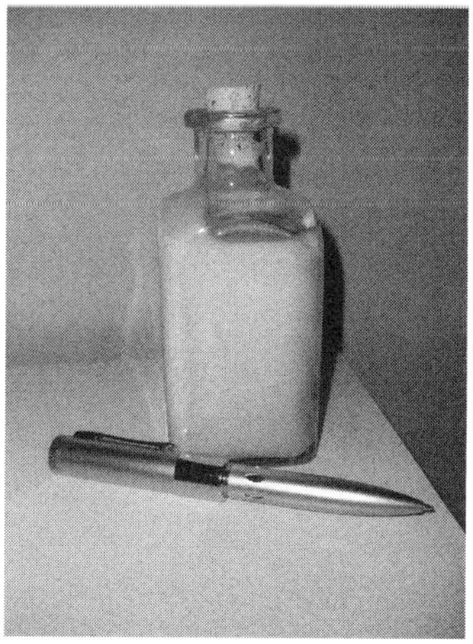

Figure 1.14 Bat blood white ink

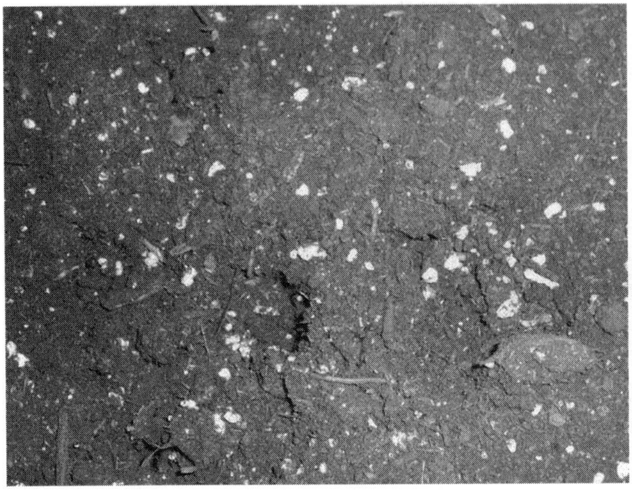

Figure 1.15 Dirt from the Grand Canyon

Dirt from the Grand Canyon

Can't get time off work? Not enough money to travel? Bid on this item and get the next best thing to actually being there – dirt from the Grand Canyon. This handful of dirt will make you the life of the party as you regale your friends with your Canyon stories. (See Figure 1.15)

Words to Put Your Baby To Sleep

The winning bidder will be emailed 25 words that have been proven to put your baby to sleep instantly. Imagine no more nights of crying and screaming – just forever bliss and peaceful slumbers. (see Figure 1.16)

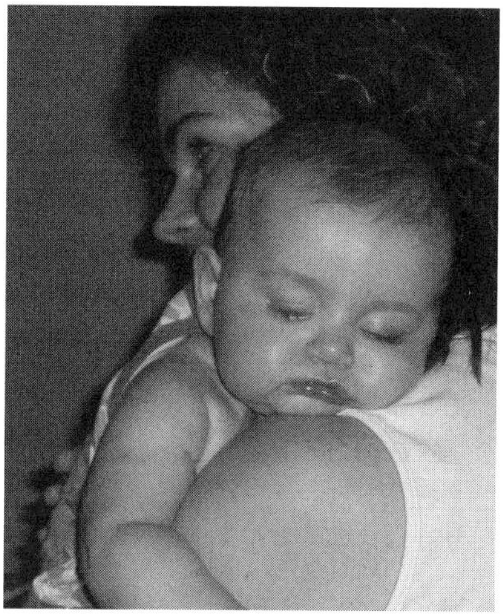

Figure 1.16 Put your baby to sleep with these words!

Are there other auction sites out there?

You better believe there are! Are any as good as eBay? That's a difficult question to answer but I can say none are more successful from a sheer numbers perspective. Let's take a look at some of the other auction sites that exist online.

Amazon.com Auctions

With international auctions sites in the United States, Japan and across Europe, Amazon is braced to become a real player in this space. Categories vary much like eBay's, to include fine wines, gems, comics, movies and books. Visit them at www.amazon.com. Scroll down to the bottom of the page and on the left hand side, click on the auctions link.

Sotheby's

Sotheby's, as everyone knows, is a noted auction house. Did you know that Sotheby's sold the first printing of the Declaration of Independence for more than $8 million.

With a turnover of approximately $2 billion per annum, Sotheby's is no stranger to the auction phenomenon. What about its Internet presence though? Has it gone online? In a way, it has. There are select items for sale from its corporate website but it also works through eBay's Live auctions service for the vast majority of its items. Visit them at www.sothebys.com.

Yahoo! Auctions

Of course! This is another very popular auction site available on the web. Similar to Amazon and eBay, Yahoo! Auctions has several international sites in the UK, the Americas, Pacific rim and several other European countries.

Buy and sell anything from antiques and art to toys and video games. This site has it all! Visit them at www.yahoo.com by clicking on the auctions link.

uBid.com

uBid.com's mission statement really says it all: uBid's mission is to be the most recognized and trusted Business-to-Consumer marketplace, consistently delivering exceptional value and service to its customers and supplier partners. This is a fantastic site that offers brand-name merchandise at deep discounts, auction start prices of $1 and warranties with mostly every sale. Visit them at www.uBid.com.

Bidz.com

This site is too cool. If you haven't noticed, every site is trying to differentiate itself from one another by offering a twist on the norm. In Bidz.com case, they offer the experience of "Live Auctions" to give you the feel and excitement of a real auction. Visit them at www.bidz.com.

Bidville.com

Bidville was created in the year 2000 by a Dr. Ed Orlando as an online auction alternative to eBay. Since then, the auction site has changed hands and now sports 1,506,353 auctions in 7,207 categories! That's not bad at all. Take a look. If you're an eBay fan, you really like this site as well. Visit them at www.bidville.com.

OnSale.com

OnSale adopted the slogan that clearly defined its mission, OnSale Brings Thrills of Auctions and Bargain Hunting Online, and that's why it is called the World's Premiere Marketplace™. How does it differ from the other sites – take a look and find out. I always say, the more the merrier. Visit them at www.onsale.com.

QXL.com

Presenting Europe's answer to online auctions: QXL.com, UK Auctions since 1997. This Pan-European online auction community offers its service in 12 countries, including Italy, Holland, Sweden and France. This site is very well respected internationally and has an incredible following in Europe. Visit them at www.qxl.com.

ScamMaster I.Q. Review

Knowledge is power in the war on scammers. Here is your chance to test your scam I.Q. against the master himself; ScamMan.

Questions

1. When did it all begin for eBay? In other words, in what year did eBay start?

2. Name two other auction sites.

3. Who is eBay's founder?

4. Which famous rock star's matches were being auctioned on eBay?

5. Someone auctioned off used ________ claiming that they had belonged to Tom Cruise.

Answers

1. 1995. 2. Sotheby's, Yahoo auctions, uBid, Bidz, Bidville, OnSale, QXL.
3. Pierre Omidyar. 4. Mick Jagger. 5. Tissues.

eBay Scams Presents

THE ADVENTURES OF

SCAMMAN

CHAPTER 2

Moving Along the eBay Way

Moving Along the eBay Way

Let's move along the eBay way and get right into the meat and potatoes of the site. Now that you have a firm grip on how it all began, what you can buy and sell, as well as what other auction sites exist, it is time to jump right in and meet the crew and learn some of the basics. In this chapter, we will:

- Meet ScamMan and his pal Scummy
- Tour eBay's User Interface
- Register on both eBay and PayPal

Introducing ScamMan & Scummy

It is important to state right up front that eBay maintains that less than one-one-hundredth of one percent of all listings are fraudulent. Translation – scamming is not a rampant problem on eBay and is not at an epidemic, crisis stage. I have to agree with them, based on my 5 years of experience on eBay, I've done alright - only falling victim two times to the dreaded scum-sucking scammers that roam the alley ways of our wonderful online auction site – eBay. With that said though, we'd be naive fools to assume we are all safe and not take preventative measures to ensure we don't fall victim – especially if it can be avoided. Hence the reason for this book. Defense! Defense! Defense! No one is going to score if you have strong defensive team.

Enter ScamMan and his buddy Scummy (see Figure 2.1). These two will be rearing their very ugly heads throughout the contents of this book. Their mission – to scam you out of your money, to steal your innocence, to kill your trust in humankind and finally, to wreck your online experiences forever. Seem extreme? Talk to people who have been scammed. A good friend of mine was scammed out of $1200.00 on eBay. Long story. Suffice to say, he no longer shops online and spreads the word to anyone who will listen.

Figure 2.1 Introducing this book's scamming mascots: ScamMan & Scummy

Keep your eyes on these two guys. They are dangerous, mischievous and can sometimes be quite charming. My goal – arm you with the necessary information, tools and wherewithal (I've always wanted to use that word!) to defend yourself against these cretins. Think of this book as your preventative medicine. Take two tablespoons (chapters) every four hours and it will cure what could ail you – online, on eBay.

It's all in the Presentation (UI)

What is a UI? UI stands for User Interface and it's everything you see on your screen when you hit eBay's site. Before we get right into scam prevention, it is of extreme importance that you know your way around this juggernaut of a website. There are so many links, bells and whistles everywhere, you can sometimes feel dazed and confused. In this section, my goal is to make you feel at ease with the areas of the user interface that I think are important.

Navigating this monster of a site will come in handy as you learn how to search, bid, buy and sell in the many chapters to come.

How do I get there?

When I said the basics – I meant the basics. For those of you new to eBay, you may be wondering how you can possibly get there. Is it far? Will you have a long way to walk? Should you pack a lunch? It's pretty straightforward, like any website you are visiting – simply type in the website address, or URL and you are off to the races.

1. Launch your preferred Internet Browser. In the following examples, I will be demonstrating the steps required using Internet Explorer 6.0.

2. Click once within your browser's web address line. The text that appears there will become highlighted.

3. Type www.ebay.com or ebay.com.

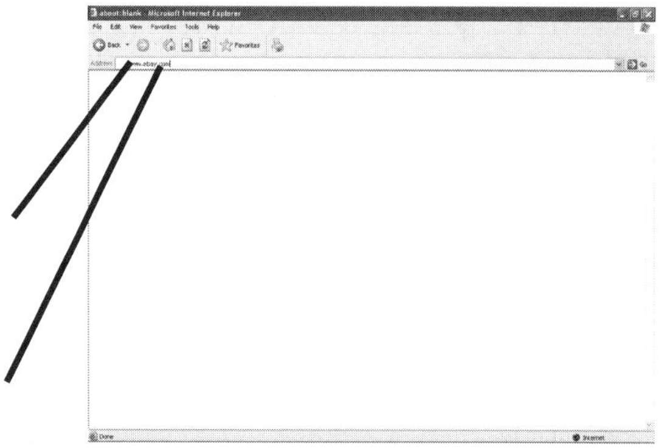

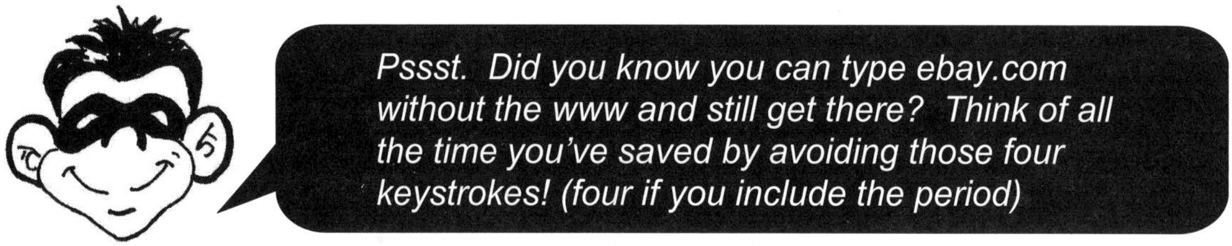

The Face of eBay

When you are greeted by eBay's front page, there are several key areas that we will be referencing in this chapter.

- eBay Toolbar
- eBay Link Bar
- Welcome New Users
- Featured Items
- Specialty Sites
- Categories
- Global Sites
- What are you looking for

Although many of these areas will be covered in more detail in various chapters later on in this book, it is still important that you are familiar with the different options available for each.

eBay Toolbar

The eBay Toolbar will become your best friend in the whole wide world. Along this toolbar are several options that will allow you to get to where you want go quickly and painlessly. Some of those options include:

- Buy. If you plan on buying things on eBay, this is a good place to start. The Buy button on the eBay Toolbar will take you to a page where everything related to buying are centrally located for easy access.

- Sell. If you plan on becoming an eBay Seller, then this is the place for you. Like the Buy page, this page includes all those things that will help you be the most effective seller on eBay.
- My eBay. Here's one of my favorite areas of eBay – the My eBay pages. Here's where you can customize a page so that it reports back to you all the things you want to track based on your eBay activity. If you are a seller, the My eBay pages will display your sales – both completed and in progress. If you are a buyer, the My eBay pages will show your purchases, bids and failed attempts. No longer just for the rich, the My eBay pages can act as your personal activity manager.
- Community. Need someone to talk to? Check out the communities on eBay. Talk shop in eBay's groups, discussion rooms and chat rooms. Get advice from the pros or simply talk to other members. This area of eBay's website serves as an excellent support resource as well.
- Help. If you couldn't find the help you need browsing the community options, then eBay's help pages are the way to go. Highly intuitive and easy to use eBay's help features are second to none in my opinion. Give them a try. You won't be disappointed.

eBay Link Bar

Ah….the eBay Link Bar. What will they think of next? Most software has menu bars but a web site? Will wonders ever cease? The eBay Link Bar, like the eBay Toolbar appears on mostly every page you visit on eBay's website. It too provides all sorts of options centralized in one handy location.

- **Home**. Need I say more? Of course! When you click on the Home link in the Link Bar, you will return to the website's front page or homepage.
- **Pay**. Pay? Pay for what? I thought it was free to use eBay. Well, it is – depending on what you are doing. More on that later but for now, the Pay link located on the Link Bar takes you to a page where you can settle up any debts you may have. We will discuss paying for items in a lot more detail in a later chapter. Stay tuned.
- **Register**. By clicking on this link, you will enter the world of eBay registration. A place where you will enter all your pertinent information and much, much more. Register not once, not twice but three times - by the time you've finished this book. Confused? Don't be. More to come on this topic!
- **Sign in/out**. Once you've registered and created your User ID and password, you will typically login or sign in to eBay to begin your buying and selling experience. This link will either take you to eBay's sign-in page or sign you out depending on what you're doing – coming or going!
- **Services**. Interesting and highly relevant! By clicking on this link, you will be transported to a page where you will find eBay's Trust, Safety, Protection and Authentication services. When you're writing a book about scams, these services will definitely come in handy.
- **Sitemap**. What is a sitemap? Have you ever wondered why these are on most websites? Looks like a page full of links? Is this supposed to be helpful? Yup. Simply put, a sitemap is a page specifically created to link all pages you want your visitors to easily find and for Search Engine robots and crawlers to index.

Welcome New Users

The Welcome New Users area of the eBay homepage is a place where novices, can quickly access useful information on various topics. Although the content in this area sometimes changes, at the time this book was written, it displayed the following options for new users to explore:

- **Buying Tips**. Click on this button and you're in for a treat as eBay propels you into a world of buying guide information. New to eBay? Fear of bidding? Scared to send money? Read the Buying Guide. You'll never fear again.
- **Track your Purchase**s. Whoaaaaa! Purchases? I just got here! Go ahead and click on this button – you won't be sorry. Put your feet up and watch the short video on My eBay. Get a feel for how My eBay can truly benefit your buying and selling experiences.
- **Register Now**. Self-explanatory right? Yet another way to quickly access eBay's Registration pages. Do you think they are trying to tell you something? Don't worry – we'll be registering soon!

Featured Items

The Featured Items area of the eBay webpage is where the elite list their items. Let's just say – it isn't free to list there and you can just imagine the type of exposure a seller would get. I think it would be safe to say that over a million people use eBay day to day. If you're item is featured on the front page – you're probably going to get some traffic. We'll look at costing out this option in a later chapter. Keep your hands on your wallet – we'll be there soon.

Specialty Sites

You would think that one site would be enough for eBay, but that is where you are wrong. In addition to eBay, there are a number of specialty sites that are advertised on eBay's homepage. They are:

- eBay Motors. Think eBay - for anything automotive. Buying a car will never be the same once you visit eBay Motors.
- eBay Stores. eBay Stores is a spot on eBay where sellers can show off all of their listings on customized pages – they create! Many of the eBay Stores offer fixed price (Buy It Now) items not available in regular search results and categories on eBay.
- Half.com by eBay. This is a fantastic site where you can purchase items at fixed prices a la Amazon.com. Owned and run by eBay, this website is a whole lot of fun to use and has a lot of great bargains too. This place is definitely worth the visit.
- PayPal. Simply put, members can send and receive money via email using PayPal service. What does this mean to you and me? As a seller – you get paid faster! As a buyer – you get your item faster! Everyone wins! More to come on PayPal and the joy and merriment it can bring to eBay members worldwide.

Categories

Categories on eBay are a great way to see just how many different types of items are actually for sale on eBay. When you browse through eBay's categories, you are really taking a walk through the world's biggest flea market, aisle by aisle, room by room. Use eBay Categories feature when you are looking for collections of like items but nothing in particular. I typically use the Categories feature when searching for DVDs in general. There, I can see all the DVDs currently for sale by genre and pick from the lot!

What are you looking for?

You're obviously looking for something right? Well – eBay is just asking you to plop it into their search box and you're off to the races. Easily the most popular area of the eBay front page. Go ahead and give it a try. You'll be amazed at how easy they've made it for you to jump right in and get started.

Global Sites

eBay continues to expand its global vision and strategy by offering country specific versions of its site like Canada, Italy, Singapore and the United Kingdom. Currently, there are over 20 different country sites available.

Helpful Links

eBay is always trying to save you time by offering useful links from their front page. The Helpful links are usually in rotation on their website so sometimes you'll see them, while other times you may not. The content of the Helpful Links section sometimes changes as well and at the time this book was written, it listed the following options:

- Learning Center. This is the mother of all help and training portals. No matter what you require assistance with, this is the place to start.
- **PayPal Buyer Protection**. By registering for this added protection through PayPal, any item you purchase on eBay using PayPal services will be protected against scammers

and fraud for up to $500.00. Read through the content on this page to get the full picture!

- **eBay Toolbar**. Not to be mistaken with the eBay toolbar that is part of user interface, the eBay Toolbar is a free downloadable tool that gives you easy, quick access to eBay from within your browser. No matter what website you are visiting, the eBay Toolbar will be visible in your Browser's user interface. Use this toolbar to track your bids, watch items and give you quick access to eBay related sites. There are too many features to list for this incredible toolbar but suffice to say – it can mean the difference between winning and losing an auction. Check it out – it's worth it.

Registering

Its time to tell eBay who you are. Registering is important on eBay because you can't buy or sell without doing it first. Let's step through the registration process and I'll do by best to share some helpful tips along the way. Tips scammers wouldn't want me sharing with you – of course!

How do I get there?

1. In your browser's address bar, type www.ebay.com.

2a. From eBay's homepage, click on the Register link on the eBay Link Bar

or

2b. From eBay's homepage, click on the Register Now button in the Welcome New Users section.

Boom! We are ready to register. Exciting isn't it? Not really – but its one of those things you have to do in life. Let's get to it.

For your Information (FYI)

Once you hit this link to register, you are presented with a page called Registration.

What do you do here? I'll give you one guess – how does enter information sound? The usual things are requested here, such as full name, street address, and phone numbers. Not much hand holding required here. As you scroll down the page, you'll notice we are getting to some more interesting fields. First, you have to enter your email address. Dog gone it! Why do I have to enter it twice? You'll notice that most sites and applications require you to enter your email address twice to ensure that you entered it right the first time.

Mumbo Jumbo

Lower on the page you will be confronted, and I do mean confronted with eBay's User Agreement and Privacy Policy page. Let's call a spade, a spade and cut right to the chase. No one reads these. No one. If you are one of the few, go ahead and skim through this exciting text, check the necessary box and slam your mouse down on the Continue button.

Pssst. In order to register, you must enter an email address that you can check right away. So don't bother entering one from work or school. Use the one you can get access to immediately.

eBay User ID

The page that follows asks you to punch in an eBay User ID. What you type here will forever be the name people see when you are buying and selling on eBay. Make it a good one. Pick one that represents who you are. If you're into selling cars, call yourself Automan500, if bowling is your thing, call yourself KingPinz. I think you're getting the picture. Or, if your preference is to be unoriginal and boring, go ahead and select one of the options provided by eBay.

Pssst. When choosing an eBay User ID, never, and I mean never, use your email address. Scammers or should I say spammers, have a real field day with unsuspecting new members who do that.

Open Sesame and Secrets Abound

Do you know where the famous saying "Open Sesame" came from? I didn't until I did some research on the topic. Open Sesame is the magical password which opened the door of the robber's den in the Arabian Nights tale of ``The Forty Thieves''. They called it a magic password. Unfortunately, on eBay – there is no such thing.

Why am I telling you this? In this section we are going to tackle the ever sensitive topic of passwords and secret questions.

Passwords

To put it mildly, Scammers love bad passwords. My job is to make a scammer's life a lot more difficult by arming you with password skills. It truly is an art and I'm the Picasso of passwords on the web. Here are some tips I've compiled that are clean and simple. Follow them – for your own good.

- Always include a numeric digit or some form of punctuation.
- Use a phrase with no spaces (e.g. Ilovemycat).
- Change it often, like your underwear. Adding a numeric digit to your password and increasing it by one each time does not constitute a valid change. Really change it – completely.
- Always use different passwords on different websites.
- Always use at least 8 characters.
- Mix it up with a blend of upper and lower case letters.
- Use multiple words strung together, separated by punctuation (i.e. D0g-c@t-$nake).
- Never use any personal information about yourself like your phone number, partner's name, kid's name or pet's name. Too obvious.
- Never use a single word that you will find in the dictionary, like cat, guitar, or rock. Too many pieces of software out there can sniff those passwords out and take you to the cleaners in the process.

If the above list seems like overkill, you're right. There is no way to implement all the rules I put together but it's a good idea to try at least one or two. Why your password is so important will be explained in a later chapter when we look at how scammers work your password to get to the gold.

Secret Question

What is the secret question? This is eBay's added security measure that allows you to accidentally forget your password and then answer this question to get a new one. Unfortunately, you can only pick from suggested questions eBay provides. Personally, I prefer creating my own secret questions but what can you do when you live in a shoe? I hate it when people say that.

Word of advice. Be tricky. If you use the question "What is your pet's name?", use your neighbors's pet's name. If you use the question "What street did you grow up on?", use your wife's street name. Bottom line – it's time for a smokescreen. It's easier than you think to steal or hijack someone's identity on eBay and run like a madman through the listings buying and selling everything in sight. More on this topic later when we discuss hijacking accounts and what you can do to protect yourself.

Ready to Roll on eBay

You've done the deed, and the worse it over. You are now ready to receive the prize – registration! Launch your email program, and there you should see an email from eBay. As the text states in the email you receive, you are almost done as you inch your mouse towards the big button that says, Complete eBay Registration.

Registering on PayPal

We looked at PayPal earlier in this chapter when we were touring eBay's user interface. If you recall, members can send and receive money via email using PayPal service. If you're a seller, you better be on PayPal because this is one of the most preferred ways buyers like to pay. If you're a buyer, you can't beat PayPal for getting your money out the door so your item gets to you quicker.

Accessing PayPal to Register

Getting there is easy. Either click on the PayPal button on eBay's front page or type www.paypal.com in your browser's address line and you are ready to go.

Once you arrive at PayPal's home page, click on the Sign Up Now button in the Member Login area and the registration process will begin.

Getting the Basics

We are going to go through the process of signing up on PayPal for a Basic User Account. There are two types of accounts to pick from: Basic and Business. The real significant difference between the two is that with a Business account, you can not only send and receive payments but as well accept credit card payments.

1. Click on the Personal Account In radio button.

2. Click on the country drop down menu and select the country from where you will be performing your transactions using PayPal.

3. Click on the Continue button.

4. Complete all your personal information in the fields provided.

5. Scroll down the page to the password and secret question area.

In this area, like eBay, you are prompted to enter a password and secret questions. The difference here is that your login name is automatically your email address and there are two secret questions as opposed to one.

1. As you scroll down the page, you will see the PayPal User Agreement and Privacy Policy. Proceed to check the appropriate options.

2. Enter what you see in the Security Measure section and you are almost done setting up your account.

3. Click on the Sign Up button.

Go check your email. PayPal has sent you one and they are waiting for you to confirm your email address, click the link within and complete your registration process.

Now you're back on PayPal's site, ready to begin your PayPal experience.

There you have it folks, registering on PayPal in ten easy steps. Wasn't that easy? Now you're ready to hit the town and impress your friends. Let them know – you're registered on both eBay and PayPal!

ScamMaster I.Q. Review

Knowledge is power in the war on scammers. Here is your chance to test your scam I.Q. against the master himself; ScamMan.

Questions

1. eBay maintains that less than ______________ of 1 percent of all listings are fraudulent.

2. What does UI stand for?

3. True or False. You can type eBay.com in your browser without the www before it?

4. What is a Sitemap?

5. The password that you create should always be at least _____ characters.

Answers

1. one-one-hundredth. 2. User Interface. 3. True. 4. A Sitemap is a page specifically created to link all pages you want your visitors to easily find and for Search Engine robots and crawlers to index. 5. Eight.

eBay Scams Presents

THE ADVENTURES OF

SCAMMAN

CHAPTER 3

Help is on the Way

Help is on the Way

Are you like most people who meet eBay for the first time? Are you trembling in your boots at the sheer size and magnitude of a site this big? Do you feel intimidated, scared and oh so alone. Don't. Help is on the way! Hence – the title of this chapter! eBay almost overdoes it when it comes to the different help and community features it offers to its users. No matter what level of eBay experience you have, these help features will surely delight and amaze.

Pssst. To avoid a boring, drawn out description of each help and community feature on eBay, I've decided to take another approach. Instead, let's look at real life examples of how each would be used. Put on your seatbelts people – bumpy ride ahead.

The Help Hub

Welcome to the Help Hub. This is your one-stop shop for all your help and community needs. Wait a minute. You may not be seeing what I'm seeing so I better slow down. To access the Help Hub, simply click on the Help button in the eBay toolbar. There – that feels better. Ahem. Welcome to the Help Hub – your new home away from home.

Search and A-Z Index

So – what's the problem? You were rolling along quite nicely when all of sudden you hit a speed bump. As you were searching for an item, you noticed all sorts of icons displayed next to the different search results. What are you going to do? Guess what each icon may mean? I think not. Let's see how using the search and index features we can get to the bottom of this eBay caper.

Using the Search

Type it in. Click Search. Done. If only getting help in real life was this easy. Let's take a look at this process step by step.

1. Click on the Help button in the eBay Toolbar. The Help Hub screen appears.

2. In the Search Help text box, type: icons

3. Click on the Search Help button. The help search results are displayed.

The results show that there are 32 possible matches for your search. After a quick scan of the results, it becomes clear which match is the best - Gift Icons in Search Results Like Bottle, Tie, Flag, Heart, and Ring.

Using the A-Z Index

For people not into searching, eBay provides an index of all the help topics available – listed from A through Z. Maybe you're not sure what the feature you're looking for is called. Maybe you're lazy and you want things laid out for you – plain and simple. Join my club then and let's take a look at the index in action.

1. Click on the Help button in the eBay Toolbar. The Help Hub screen appears.

2. Click on the A-Z Index located on the left side of the page.

3. From the alphabet of letters that appears at the top of the page, click on the letter "i" for icons.

4. Right at the top of the list is a help topic called: Icons in Listings.

5. Click on the Icons in Listings link. Help on icon listings is displayed.

Now that was easy, right! Could it get any easier? These are, by far my two preferred ways of searching on eBay. Didn't I tell you that help would be on the way!

Contact Us

Let's take a look at different forms of help that you may require. If after searching through the topics and index you are unable to find what you are looking for, eBay provides a Contact Us feature. Using this link, you can send your question directly to helpful eBay staff who will be more than happy to assist you. Let's take a look at an example of this feature in action.

Let's say you've come across a scammer who is attempting to spoof you. What does spoof mean? Sometimes, scammers will send you emails pretending to be an eBay representative. They've designed the email and associated website so well, that you could swear it really was eBay sending that message. Their goal is to swindle you out of your password, user IDs or credit card information. These fraudulent emails and websites are sometimes called "spoofed" or "spoof" sites. Your goal is to report them. Using the Contact Us link, help is on the way.

1. Click on the Help button in the eBay Toolbar. The Help Hub screen appears.

2. Click on the Contact Us link located on the left side of the page.

3. From the list of options that appears, click on the *Report Fake eBay emails (spoofs) and unauthorized account activity* link.

4. The screen will refresh and more categories will appear below the first set.

5. From the new list, click on the *Fake or suspicious eBay email* link.

6. The screen will refresh and more categories will appear below the second set.

7. From the new list, choose the link that applies most appropriately. In this example, because you have already read through this book from cover to cover, you selected the *You received an eBay email that may be fake* link (instead of the "after the fact" option entitled *You replied to an email requesting personal data and you can't access your account.*)

8. Click on the Continue button.

9. On the following page, you are given the option to either click on an instant help topic, like *How do I know that an email is really from eBay?* or go ahead and contact eBay with the specifics.

That's the Contact Us link in full effect. eBay claims that they will respond to your queries and issues within 24 to 48 hours. In my experience, their response time has been even better. If you have a question that's not answered on their site or you have an infraction to report, go no further – help is definitely on the way!

Learning Center

If you're new to eBay or if you need a quick refresher, the Learning Center is definitely the place to be. Packed full of informative videos called courses, there's a whole lot of learning to be had. The topics range from buying to selling to searching and bidding. Live example ahead!

Scared of bidding? Not sure how to do it? What if a seller gets mad at me for being a stupid bidder? Why not visit the Learning Center and actually run through an interactive bidding exercise. Let's run through the steps to get there.

1. Click on the Help button in the eBay Toolbar. The Help Hub screen appears.

2. Click on the Learning Center link in the Related Links section.

3. Click on the How to Buy link in the Choose a Topic section of the page. Several learning options are displayed.

4. Click on the "Try a Practice Bid" link.

That's it. The rest is magic. Using these screens as practice, you can go through the exercise of entering test bids, outbidding and being outbid all in the comfort and safety of a pseudo eBay environment.

If you'd rather sit back and be taught rather than having to interact, audio tours are just what the doctor ordered.

1. Click on the Help button in the eBay Toolbar. The Help Hub screen appears.

2. Click on the Learning Center link in the Related Links section. The Learning Center page appears.

3. Click on the How to Buy link in the Choose a Topic section of the page. Several learning options are displayed.

4. Click on the How to Bid and Buy Audio Tour link.

Like a movie playing on your computer, the audio tour will step you through the bidding and buying process. By the way, did I mention that you control the speed of the course by using the handy dandy playback controls! I didn't? Now you know!

eBay University

Dropped out of high school? Never completed university? No worries. eBay University is now open and accepting enrollments. Bring your pen, pad and don't forget your wallet – most of this stuff ain't free!

Looking to go beyond the basics? Are you looking for live instruction on how to make a business out of your eBay sales? Follow the leader as I guide you through the enrollment process at eBay University.

1. Click on the Help button in the eBay Toolbar. The Help Hub screen appears.

2. Click on the eBay University link in the Related Links section of the page.

3. Click on the Learn More link in the eBay University classroom instruction section of the page.

4. Scroll down until you see the Beyond the Basics course description.

5. Click on the Choose City drop down menu and select your desired class location.

6. Details, times and location will be displayed for the selected city.

You are ready to be taught by eBay's expert instructors. Many are accomplished authors, eBay employees or just plain experts in the field. If you've got the cash, you are ready to learn from the pros!

eBay Security Center

Someone after you? Do you feel like someone is trying to steal your confidential information? Maybe you have a feeling that you're being spoofed by a scammer. Enter the eBay Security Center. Think Superman without the cape. As eBay puts it, the Security Center is designed to be your single source for direct, actionable information about safety and security in the eBay marketplace.

Looking for tips on how to protect your eBay account information? Hold my hand as I guide you through the caverns of the eBay Security Center.

1. Click on the Help button in the eBay Toolbar. The Help Hub screen appears.

2. Click on the Security Center link in the Related Links section of the page.

3. Click on the Protecting your eBay Account link.

Give that page a read. It provides very helpful steps as to what you can do if you suspect your account has been compromised in any way.

The eBay Security Center also offers tips on buying, selling and paying safely. This content absolutely compliments the advice given in this book. I strongly recommend taking the time to read through these sections. Consider it time well spent – especially if you're serious about your time on eBay.

Communities

Welcome to the eBay Community. We just finished discussing all the fantastic help features that eBay provides its users. Now, we are going to discuss all the fun, informative and exciting people you can meet on eBay. Using the Communities, you can talk to other members and eBay staff, read the eBay news, learn about eBay events and meet lots of new people.

Talk

Like to talk like I do? Then this section of the eBay communities page is definitely for you.

Discussion Board & Chat Rooms

Many of you are probably already familiar with discussion boards and chat rooms. Well, eBay has its own. If you'd like to talk to people like you about topics you are about, you can use eBay's discussion board and chat rooms to get your comments out to the masses.

In this example, I've got something to say about scammers and escrow sites. Let's take a look at how I would go about posting a message to the discussion board regarding this topic.

1. Click on the Community button on the eBay toolbar.

2. In the Talk box, click on the Discussion Boards link. Lists of category boards are displayed.

3. Click on the escrow/insurance link, located in the leftmost column of topics.

Welcome to the Escrow/Insurance Discussion Board. Here, I can begin a new thread where I introduce all the fraudulent escrow sites I know of. I can even solicit others to add to my list creating a comprehensive list of spoof escrow sites. Discussion Boards are definitely the way to go when seeking or sharing information with the eBay masses.

Answer Center

In the Talk section, you will also find an option for the Answer Center. This is a member to member question and answer board chock full of information. Scan through the different questions by topic of interest and take a look at all the responses. If we wanted to go about posting a question in the Answer Center about PayPal, here's how we would do it:

1. Click on the Community button on the eBay toolbar.

2. In the Talk box, click on the Answer Center link. Lists of Question and Answer boards are displayed.

3. Click on the PayPal link, located in the rightmost column of board topics.

When I last checked, there was over 550 pages of questions related to PayPal listed on this board. Can you believe it? You'd be hard pressed not to find the question you probably wanted to ask already in there. Take a look by eyeballing the pages or do it the smart way – use the built-in search feature for that page.

News

Extra, extra, read all about it! eBay news hot off the presses! When you visit the Communities page, you will also see an option for News as it relates to General Announcements, System Announcements and something eBay calls "The Chatter". Let's take a closer look.

General Announcements

On the General Announcements page, you'll find all the latest buzz around anything and everything that is eBay. If there's a special promotion on for new star spangled borders for your listings – you'll find it here. If eBay is merging with Victoria Secret, you'll hear about it here. I think you get the picture. Stay current and impress your friends by reading the General Announcement pages.

System Announcements

Contrary to popular opinion, eBay is not Superman. It has to take a break from time to time and recharge its batteries. When you visit the System Announcements pages, you will be kept up to date on eBay's scheduled maintenance periods. An example of an announcement would be as follows on the next page.

> ***Scheduled Maintenance for October 22nd***
>
> Date: 10/20/04 Time: 03:18:10 PM PDT
>
> The eBay system will be undergoing general maintenance from approximately 01:00 to 03:00 PT on Friday, October 22nd. During this maintenance period, certain eBay site features may be intermittently unavailable or slow.
>
> Regards,
>
> eBay

The Chatter

Enough suspense already – what is "The Chatter". The Chatter is an online newsletter all about the wacky people and events that make up eBay. It's a great read and really entertaining. Think of it as a one-stop shop of eBay news and grooves for people wanting to be "in the know" about eBay.

Events

If you ever wanted to have a calendar view of all the different events occurring at any given time – look no further. The Events link found on the Communities page displays a schedule of events with live links to further details. It's a great way to get a bird's eye view of what's happening across the eBay space. If you're lucky, eBay may be coming to a hotel near you really soon.

People

On the People pages you will find features that allow you create groups, read about eBay's value system and last but not least, check out the member spotlight area. These pages make me feel very warm inside.

Groups

Using groups, members can create special interest communities where people can participate in discussions, read newsletters, conduct polls, view calendars and share photo albums. The following steps detail how an individual can create their own group on eBay.

1. Click on the Community button on the eBay toolbar.

2. In the People box, click on the eBay Groups link. The Group Center is displayed.

Pssst. In order to start a new group, you must be a registered member on eBay for at least 90 days and have a minimum of 50 feedback points.

3. Click on the Start Group link.

Values

You probably won't venture into the Values section of the People area so I thought I would pull it and print it here for you to read. It outlines eBay's five fundamental values. Values I believe should govern our lives outside of eBay – as well.

eBay is a community that encourages open and honest communication among all its members. Our community is guided by five fundamental values:

- We believe people are basically good.
- We believe everyone has something to contribute.
- We believe that an honest, open environment can bring out the best in people.
- We recognize and respect everyone as a unique individual.
- We encourage you to treat others the way you want to be treated.

eBay is firmly committed to these principles. And we believe that community members should also honor them—whether buying, selling, or chatting with eBay friends.

Now - those are words to live by.

Member Spotlight

Find out how the rest of us live – on eBay! Members recount stories of fame and fortune, reveal insights into what makes their eBay clocks tick and how they got started. Get to know other members intimately by taking a look at the member spotlight.

In case you were curious, only members with a minimum of 100 feedback points and at least a 98% positive feedback rating can apply to be in the spotlight.

ScamMaster I.Q. Review

Knowledge is power in the war on scammers. Here is your chance to test your scam I.Q. against the master himself; ScamMan.

Questions

1. To access the Help Hub, simply click on the ____ button in the eBay toolbar.

2. Which link allows you to send your question directly to helpful eBay staff who will be more than happy to assist you?

3. Which features allows you to watch videos called courses to help you learn about using eBay?

4. ____ ________ provides you with live instruction on how to make a business out of your eBay sales.

5. Which section of eBay is designed to be your single source for direct, actionable information about safety and security in the eBay marketplace?

Answers

1. Help. 2. Contact Us. 3. Learning Center. 4. eBay University.
5. Security Center.

eBay Scams Presents

THE ADVENTURES OF

SCAMMAN

CHAPTER 4

The Art of the Search

The Art of the Search

Is there really an art to searching? Couldn't anyone waltz up to eBay, plop in something they are looking for and be done with it? The answer to that question is yes. The more important question though is "Will it be the most effective search?". Probably not. Before you can bid or buy anything, you have to find that "anything". Let the treasure hunt begin!

In this chapter we will look at:

- Basic Searches
- Advanced Searches
- Category Browsing
- Favorite Searches

Basically, Just Searching!

What are you looking for? That is the question. When you come to eBay's home page, you're going to feel somewhat inundated with all the bells and whistles going off all over the screen. Nestled quite snugly near the top of this page you will see a "What are you looking for?" search text box. This is eBay's sweet spot – so to speak. It is from here that you will be conducting most of your searches.

I had mentioned in my introduction that anyone can come to eBay's homepage, plop in some text and find what they are looking for using this search box. It's fast and it's definitely easy. Using this method, you can't always be sure that you're getting the best results though. Regardless, let's put this search tool to use.

1. In your browser's address bar, type: www.ebay.com

2. Click once within the "What are you looking for?" search text box.

3. Type the item you are looking for, i.e. sea monkeys

4. Click on Find It.

Advanced Searches

What comes next depends on how good your search criteria was in the first place. I pride myself on being able find anything and everything on eBay. If someone were to approach me and say they can't find a certain something - I take it as a challenge. I will find it. The problem with the "What are you looking for?" search box is that it doesn't really scream of search options. It's meant to be plain and simple. eBay also offers more advanced search capabilities or "smart searches" as they like to call them. Let's take a closer look at these options.

Finding Items

By default, when you click on the Smart Search link or the Advanced Search link, you will come to the Find Items page. Here, there are many things you can do to refine your search criteria. Let's use the following example. My brother is looking for some baseball cards he used to have when he was a kid. All he remembers is that they were cartoon pictures of players, each player was a monster and he believes the word freaks or freaky was in the title. That's not a lot to work with but I love the challenge.

1. From eBay homepage, I clicked on the Smart Search link located just below the What are you looking for? Search text box. The Find Items page is displayed.

2. In the "Enter keyword or item number" text box, I typed the following keywords: freaks baseball card monster.

3. In the category drop down, I selected Sports Mem, Cards & Fan Shop.

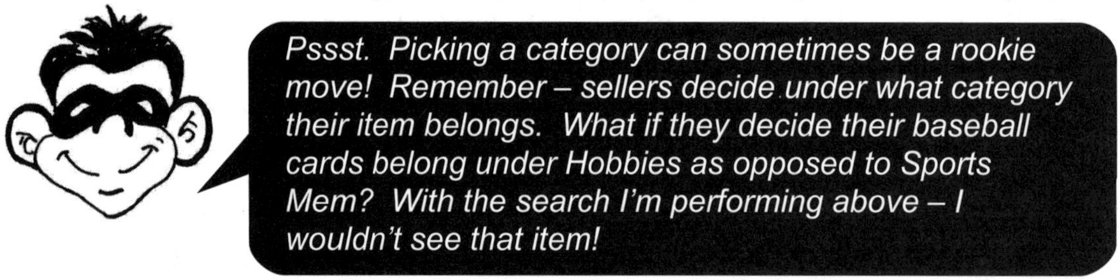

4. I then clicked on Search. The results of this search were abysmal. One result. My brother was not going to be happy. It's time to pull out the little guns. I say little guns because the big guns come out a little later. This is getting personal.

5. I returned to the Find Items search page (using the Browser back button).

6. Using the same search criteria selected earlier, I enabled the "Search title and description" check box. That's the search secret weapon. With this feature enabled, you are not only finding those keywords in the title of a listing but as well in the body of the description. This feature is best used for items you may not remember much about – like freak baseball cards with monsters for example (yeesh).

7. I clicked on Search. This time I came up with more results but they weren't relevant. A bunch of XBox results showed up. What's a guy to do? Go talk to his brother. After speaking with my brother some more, he revealed one more juicy tidbit that I was sure was going to help me with my search – the manufacturer name! The name of the company that put these cards out was Donruss. With this additional piece of the puzzle, I was confident I would get more results.

8. In the "Enter keyword or item number" text box, I retyped the following keywords: freaks donruss baseball. I kept the "Search title and description" check box checked for this search.

Pssst. Remember – sometimes less is more – especially when searching. Sure, it's great form to include all the keywords you know for a certain item but keep in mind, if it isn't a perfect match to the seller's title/description – nothing will come up.

9. I clicked on Search. Jackpot! Four results were displayed. Looks like these were rarer than I thought. Created in the eighties, these cards are apparently real collector's editions. Happy with my results, I let my brother know how I made out. Would he bid? Would he be happy? Let's find out.

In terms of housekeeping, let's quickly define three more options that appear on the Find Items page. These features only effect how your results will be displayed.

- Sort By. Using the sort by drop down, you can control in what order your results appear. For example, you can display your results from the highest price to the lowest or vice versa.

- View Results. Using this drop down menu, you can control what view your results will have. Here, you can select from Gallery view (picture gallery view), All Items view and Show Item Number.
- Results per page. Simply put – this lets you control how many results you'll see per page.

Now, with the housekeeping out of the way, let's find out what my brother had to say regarding my search prowess.

Completed Listing Only

You may have noticed a feature called "Completed listings only" located on the Find Items page. With this feature enabled, only those auctions that have past will be displayed. Why would anyone want to see completed auctions? You can't bid anymore – the bar's closed! I'll tell you why - people like my brother.

When I let him know that I found his items for sale. He was jubilant. He did have some reservations though. He was wondering if I could tell him how high I think the bidding would go for these items. How would I know? Very easily. Using the Completed Listing Only feature, I can look at past auctions and see just how high these auctions have gone. This would give my brother an indication as to what he may be in for and how thick his wallet would have to be. Here's what I did:

10. I enabled the Completed Listing Only check box on the Find Items page.

11. Using the same search criteria as entered and selected previously, I clicked on Search.

Only three items were displayed and of the three, only one sold for $3.99. Granted, it was only a wrapper and not the actual cards that sold. This was not going to help my brother except to say, no one was bidding at all. That can be a good thing. I shooed my brother along. On to the next example.

More Advanced Search Options

On the Find Items page, there's a rather innocent looking link situated just to the right of the search button. The name of this link is, More search options. Go ahead, don't be afraid – click on it! Boooom! Have you ever seen so many search options in your life? Let's observe some of these search options in action using a real life example.

My wife is a huge fan of Ali G. If you don't know who he, run a Google search. He's one funny guy. My wife was looking to buy the latest release of the Ali G movie on DVD but she had no idea what it was called. Enter – the Search King. That's right – me!. There's the wrong way to search and there's the right way. I suggested she follow my lead. She wasn't a big fan of following anything I do but she agreed and became Gabriel's pupil.

1. In the "Enter keyword or item number" text box, I typed the following keywords: Ali G movie. To really make sure I found what she was looking for (she has a real mean left hook), I enabled the "Search title and description" check box for this search.

2. I left the category drop-down set to All Categories to really ensure something came back.

3. Just below the Search title and description feature is a drop-down menu that allows me to control how my keywords are searched on. For example, you can select from the

following options: All of these words, Any of these words, Exact Phrase and Exact Match. I left it set to the default position: All of these words. This tells eBay that I am only interested in results that include all three of my keywords.

Feeling cocky, I slammed my mouse down on the Search button anticipating success and riches. Instead, I had over 149 results, many of which were not even close. Where did I go wrong? I know. I shouldn't of enabled the Search title and description feature. Let's try again.

With the Search title and description feature disabled, I re-ran my search. This time, the results were definitely somewhat more manageable – but not perfect (my wife nagged in my ear). Twenty four results were returned based on my search criteria. It was time to bring out the big guns and really search this baby down.

Looking at the 24 search results, I noticed that there were not only movies listed but posters and box sets as well. I knew my wife wasn't interested in the those items so I wanted to remove them from my results. I also knew that my wife only wanted to spend between ten and twenty dollars on this DVD. Last but not least, I knew she would only want to pay by PayPal. She doesn't trust any other method. Wheew. That's a lot of criteria. Do you think eBay can handle it? You know they can.

4. On the Find Items page (More Search Options displayed), I located the Exclude Words text box. There, I typed poster and set. This would remove any of those results that included those keywords.

Before I hit the Search button though, I had some other business to take care of.

5. Further down the Find Items page, I clicked within the Items Priced text boxes. There, I typed in ten and twenty for min and max values. That will keep her in budget!

Pssst. These values only address the bid price at that current "search" time. Obviously, once the bidding begins, those prices can surpass your maximum bid amount.

6. Last but not least, further down the Find Items page, there is an option to only display Items listed with PayPal. I selected it.

Now, the moment of truth. Drum roll please. I hit the Search button and the results were magical! Three results were displayed, each matching my wife's criteria – exactly! The kisses just kept coming after that. I have to do searches for her more often!

To collapse the More Search Options page, simply click on the link located at the bottom of the Find Items page called: Fewer Search Options. That's just what I did.

Items by Seller

On the Advanced Search page, you'll also notice an option to search for items by seller. With this link selected, your search options change. Simply put, using this search feature, you can display all the items a particular seller is selling and no one else's.

Like any store where you get great service, you usually come back for more. Well, on eBay, this rule seems to ring true as well. In light of all the possible scams out there, many people aren't comfortable just dealing with anyone. Maybe there's a seller you've dealt with who gave you excellent customer service. Maybe there's a seller out there who you've really grown to trust. If that's the case, by searching by seller, you can see all of their current or even completed auctions at any given time.

Items by Bidder

This search option is a real winner and really fitting for this book. If you're a seller and you feel like you may be falling victim to a scam, finding items by bidder may be your ticket. When members are bidding on your item for sale, their user IDs are listed along the way. You can take any one of their user IDs, punch them into the "Enter Bidder's User ID" text box and you are off to the races. This will display all of the auctions that bidder has bid on over the past 30 days (including completed items). Wave goodbye to shillers, shielders and phantoms. When you get through some of the scam chapters later on in this book, you'll really understand how this search page can help you bust some scams.

By Item Number

Last but not least, if you ever needed to search for an item by item number, you can use this search page. Options include finding the actual item listing or location.

Items in Stores

What's the main difference between buying an item from your average seller and buying an item from store? eBay Stores allows members to show you all of their listings and promote their business all through their own customized pages. eBay Stores typically offer Store Inventory items which are additional fixed priced items not available by regular search channels. Searching in eBay Stores will bring you results that you wouldn't normally get otherwise. That's good enough for me.

The Items in Store search options are exactly the same as the Find Items pages except for the inclusion of Store Inventory. By enabling the Search Store Inventory items only feature, only those items not available through other search methods will be displayed. That's one of the main benefits of using this search page.

Find Stores

Do you like dealing with stores rather than your Joe or Jill seller? Well, if yes was your answer to that question, you'll love this search page. A friend of mine loves shopping the eBay Stores. He swears by it and wouldn't shop on eBay any other way. One day recently, he was looking for eBay Stores that sold silver age comic books. He was especially looking for Green Lantern #40 from 1965. Here's what he did, using this search page.

1. On the eBay "Smart Search" page, he clicked on the Find Stores link. The Find Stores page is displayed.

2. In the "Enter keywords or Store name" search text box, he typed: silver age comics.

3. He enabled the "Stores with matching items" option. With this option selected, only stores that actually sold silver age comics would be displayed.

4. He then clicked on the Search button.

Over fifty results came streaming back. That's a lot of stores selling silver age comic books. Well, my friend wasn't complaining as he clicked through their stock like a madman.

Find a Member

In the Members section of the eBay Smart Search pages, you can find a member by user ID, in order to see their Feedback, About Me page, or User ID history. This is a great feature to use when you are investigating a bidder, buyer or seller. By punching in their user ID, you can quickly get to their feedback comments (spot the negatives), About Me Page (see who they are and what they are all about) and their User ID history (tells you if they have been changing them up like underwear).

Find Contact

Using this search page, members are able to request another member's contact information. This feature is pretty scary considering some of the scams you're going to read about in later chapters. To prevent fraudsters from abusing the use of this search page, eBay includes a safeguard. You can only request contact information if you are involved in a current or recent transaction with that member. You are also prompted to enter the item number of the item you are trading with said member.

Find User ID

You can also track down a member's user ID if you already have their email address. Again, this is a scammer's dream page to work from. eBay has put the proper safeguards in place as well for this feature. Like the search page before it, you can only request user ID information if you are involved in a current or recent transaction with that member. Over and above this safeguard, to avoid any automated bots from attacking this search page, eBay has also included an image number. Bots can't read images, only humans can. eBay asks that any member using this search page, enter what they see in that image number to ward off scammers.

Categorically Speaking

Another way of searching on eBay is to not search at all – but instead – browse! Using eBay's categories, you can browse through like collections of items and select what you like rather than searching for a specific thing. The best example that comes to mind when I think of the advantages of category browsing is as follows:

I am a major DVD psychotic. I am constantly purchasing DVDs and I'm not above buying multiple versions of the same title if different versions are released. Be it a special, ultra special, extended, uncut, director's cut, original, or anniversary release – it has to be mine. With all that being said, I sometimes have no idea what I'm looking for. All I care about is that it's a DVD – title is secondary.

Using eBay's category browsing features, here's how I start my day on eBay.

1. From the eBay home page, I click on the DVDs and Movies link located along the left side of the page.

2. From the different sub categories shown, I click on the DVDs link.

Pssst. If you scroll down on this page, you'll see eBay's top 10 list of movies selling on eBay. At the time I was writing this book, the Star Wars Trilogy DVD set was number one. I'm a proud owner! Are you?

Its at this point where you might think I'm even crazier than you originally thought. Over 200,000 DVD results are displayed. Browsing using the category feature doesn't stop here though. I would never leave you hanging with that many results. You'd be browsing for days.

3. On the left side of the page, you'll see a list of different browse and search options. I click on the New link to ensure I only see results where sealed DVDs are being sold. Now my results are just over 150,000. We're getting there.

4. Further down the page, you will see different search options (similar to those we saw on the Find Items pages). I only deal with sellers who support PayPal payments so I enable the Items listed with PayPal option. I then click on the Show Items button to display my new set of results. Now my results are just over 140,000. That's a little better. Almost there.

5. Not a guy who typically likes to get hung up on genres, I bite the bullet and select my favorite genre of the day. Today, my fave is Documentary. With just under 4000 results to skim through, things are really coming together.

6. Here's where I pull a rabbit out of my hat. The next step is my secret weapon and I encourage you to keep it between you, me and the rest of the people reading this book. Wander quietly over to the right side of the page. There, you will see a Sort By drop-down menu. Click on the drop-down menu and select Time: Ending Soonest.

Now look at what we've done! Displayed for us all to see are all the DVD auctions ending within seconds, minutes, hours and days (in that order). If you're an impulse buyer like me and price is a big factor in your purchasing decisions, then this style of browsing is definitely the way to go. Have fun.

Favorite Searches

Now that we've learned how to search and browse, let's figure out ways we can cut down on all the labor and save ourselves some time in the process. eBay includes a feature that allows members to save favorite searches so you don't have to enter them over and over again.

In the case of the Ali G movie example I discussed earlier, that was a lot of setup to come to those results. Let's say my wife wasn't lucky enough to find the movie she wanted. Would I have to retype all that criteria each time I wanted to search. Nope. Here's how it works.

In the Ali G example, my wife had stipulated the following criteria:

Show only: Items listed with PayPal, Min Price: $10.00, Max Price: $20.00, keywords: Ali G movie, excluding set and poster.

After punching in all this information as we did in the Find Items page, we proceed as before. We would slam the search button and see our results. To save the search, a link will be displayed in the top right corner of the results page called "Add to Favorites".

When you click on this link, the Add to My Favorite Searches page appears. Here, you can give the search a name and set how long you want it to last. eBay will automatically search each day for that item and alert you by email when something comes up that matches your criteria. Now that's a time saver!

Pssst. You can access Shortcuts to Favorite Searches from eBay's homepage. If you scroll down to the bottom of the page you'll see a drop-down menu from where you can select your searches for quick access.

ScamMaster I.Q. Review

Knowledge is power in the war on scammers. Here is your chance to test your scam I.Q. against the master himself; ScamMan.

Questions

1. Where are you taken if you click on the Smart Search or Advanced Search link?

2. Why is Searching by Category an ineffective method of finding exactly what you are looking for?

3. Using the ____ ____ drop down, you can control in what order your results appear.

4. Why would you search Items by Seller?

5. True or False. You can access Shortcuts to Favorite Searches from eBay's homepage.

Answers

1. Find Items Page. 2. The sellers decide under what category their item belongs. 3. Sort By. 4. You trust the seller or have had previous dealings. 5. True.

eBay Scams Presents

THE ADVENTURES OF

SCAMMAN

CHAPTER 5

Bidding and Buying

Bidding and Buying

You've done the search. You think you've found what you are looking for. Now what? You have two choices (depending on the type of auction it is): Bid or Buy It Now. Wait a minute! We're getting ahead of ourselves again. How can we possibly go to bid or buy it now, when we have no idea what it is we are looking at. Let's get organized people and get a grip on what's required when you want to bid and buy on eBay. In this chapter, you will learn about:

- The Item View Page
- Bidding Strategies (nothing fancy)
- What to do when you win?
- What to do when you lose?

The Item View Page

Understanding your surroundings is a very important first step before you make the decision to bid or buy. Before we bid or buy, we need to understand what makes the Item Page tick. Let's take a look.

Seller Information

Alert, Alert, Alert! Very important information ahead! The Seller Information box, included on every Item Page, provides a potential bidder or buyer with extremely valuable data. Sometimes, the information contained there can mean the difference between getting scammed or having a positive transaction. Let's take a look at each component within the Seller Information box and really point out any information worth noting.

Here's a typical example of some of the information that would be contained in an Item Page's Seller Information box:

> ScamMan (5236) ★
>
> Feedback Score: 5236
> Positive Feedback: 45.8%
> Member since Nov-19-04 in United States
>
> Read feedback comments
> Add to Favorite Sellers
> Ask seller a question
> View seller's other items

On the first line, we see the seller's User ID – ScamMan (hardly a name you can trust). Next to his User ID, you will see a number enclosed in brackets. This is the same number as the one listed below it, which is the seller's Feedback Score.

The User ID and the Feedback score are both links you can click on. When you do, you are taken to that seller's feedback forum. There, you will see all the information related to that seller's previous transactions. In the case of ScamMan, by clicking on his link, you will see comments from over 5000 people who have dealt with him in the past. Those comments can be either positive, neutral or negative.

Below the Positive Feedback percentage, you will see "Member since Nov-19-04 in United States". Quite obviously, this tells us how long the seller has been "in business" so to speak.

Pssst. It is imperative that before you bid or buy an item from any seller, you click on their User ID or Feedback Points to visit their Feedback Forum. There, you should scrutinize a random sampling of the comments left for that seller. To put things in perspective, I would never deal with ScamMan based on his low percentage of positive feedback. Some buyers won't even deal with a seller with one negative feedback comment.

Further down in the Seller Information box are the following links:

- Read feedback comments. This link will take you directly to that seller's feedback comments.
- Add to Favorite Sellers. If this is a seller you like dealing with, by all means, add them as a Favorite Seller. This allows you to quickly access this seller's items from either eBay's homepage or your My eBay pages.
- Ask seller a question. Worth its weight in gold, this feature allows you to contact the seller with any questions you may have.
- View seller's other items. By clicking on this link, you can quickly see what other items a seller has for sale at that time, on eBay.

Bid & Locations Area

To the left of the Seller Information box, you will see another very important part of the Item Page. This is where you will see the item's bid or purchase price. You will also find out how many bidders are actually bidding, how much time is left in the auction and where the item is located.

Here's a typical example of content within this area of the Item Page view.

Starting bid: US $21.99

Place Bid

Time left: 57 mins 40 secs

1-day listing

Ends Oct-28-04 09:34:43 PDT

Start time: Oct-27-04 09:34:43 PDT

History: 0 bids

Price: US $26.99

Buy It Now

Item location: ScamLand

United States

Ships to: Worldwide

Shipping costs: Please contact me for shipping details

Pssst. Scammers typically create several user IDs to mask their activities. Sellers who have been members for a short time (i.e. less than a month) can sometimes be slipped into the "questionable" pile. I am not for one second saying avoid all new sellers because that's not fair at all. All I am saying is be extra careful when dealing with new sellers for that reason.

The starting bid, currently set at $21.99 is the opening bid for this item. Do we have any takers? If we did, you would simply click on the Place Bid button below it, and the fun would be begin.

The Time left lets you know exactly how much time remains in this auction.

Scammers or should I say, master bidders, will sometimes use this information as a powerful weapon. Snipers will wait until the very last seconds to bid in hopes of winning the auction. They typically keep their eyes fixed on the Time left clock.

The following three lines (shown in the following box) are fairly self-explanatory. For this item, the auction duration set by the seller is a 1-day auction (as opposed to 3, 5, 7 or 10 days). The start and end times will tell you exactly when the seller placed the listing and when it will expire based on the eBay clock.

1-day listing

Ends Oct-28-04 09:34:43 PDT

Start time: Oct-27-04 09:34:43 PDT

The next line down is the Bid History link. This link can also provide some valuable information to a potential bidder. If you're a seller, you can use this link to see exactly who is bidding on your item and what their feedback profile is. If you're a bidder, you can see exactly who is bidding against you and also check their feedback profiles.

History: 0 bids

If you're a bidder, and you want to guard against a potential shill or phantom bidding situation, bid history is a great tool to use. As a seller, you can also use this feature to detect any bid shielding action. If any of these terms are Greek to you, please refer to the scam chapters later on in this book for more information.

Pssst. The Buy It Now option is only available if no one has bid on the item yet. The moment the first bid comes through on an item, the Buy It Now feature is disabled.

Located just below the bid history link is the Buy It Now information for this item. Not all listings support this option. Simply put, this seller is offering this item at a fixed price for those who are either in a hurry or have a fear of bidding. For this example, the Buy It Now price is $26.99. If you were to click the Buy It Now button, you would be purchasing this item outright without going through the bid process.

Price: US $26.99

Buy It Now

Directly below the Buy It Now information is the item and seller's location and shipping information.

Item location: ScamLand

United States

Ships to: Worldwide

Shipping costs: Please contact me for shipping details

In this example, the item location is in a town called ScamLand (not a place I would trust typically) in the United States. This seller is willing to ship worldwide and prefers that he is contacted directly by email (using the Ask the Seller a Question link) to get accurate shipping costs.

Pssst. The Scam-Factor for this area of the item page is high. Bells and sirens should be going off left and right at this point. Here are some things to look out for in order to avoid falling victim to a scammer. With Item location, always make sure that when you are sending payment, the location in the listing matches up with the payment address the seller is giving you. Otherwise, you may be dealing with a scammer.

Last but not least, when a seller asks you to contact them for shipping costs, really make sure that you do. Sometimes (and I do mean sometimes), sellers will do this in hopes that you don't actually ask. Then, when the time comes and you've won the auction, they can charge you an arm, leg and pair of Nike shoes for shipping and handling costs. Make sure that you ask up-front – before you bid!

Description

The item description for the listing describes exactly what it is you are purchasing. Depending on the type of seller, descriptions can truly vary in terms of their design, content and accuracy (unfortunately). Typically, an item description should include everything from color and size to condition and year of manufacture. Due to the fact that there aren't any steadfast rules or policies that govern what has to be included, we can sometimes find ourselves in precarious situations. Bottom line - scammers will use the item description section to sometimes mislead bidder and buyers.

Pssst. Simply put – read everything very carefully. Look very closely at the small print – especially. Look for hidden costs that the seller may be trying to conceal at a small point size. If you find any pertinent information missing from the description, do not hesitate to contact the seller to ask.

Photos

Somewhere in the listing, you will typically see one or more photos of the item you are planning to bid on. If the listing does not have a photo, most bidders move on to the next option in their search results. Personally, if I can't see it – I'm not bidding. The best kind of photos in a listing are those that are actual shots of that item rather than a manufacturer's photo.

It is very easy to "steal" images from the web or even another listing on eBay. If you have any doubts regarding an image you see in a listing, it is not uncommon to contact the seller and request additional photos. I do it all the time. Bottom line here is that you want to ensure that the seller really has the item they are attempting to sell.

Payment methods accepted

In this section of the Item Page, you will see which payment methods the seller accepts. This can include any of the following options:

- Credit Card Payments
- Check or Money Order
- Wire Transfers

- PayPal
- BidPay
- Cash
- Other

As a seller, the more options you offer, the better chances your item will sell to a larger audience. Personally, I won't bid on any item that doesn't support PayPal payments. Its quick and easy and I get my item a lot faster.

You should also avoid wire transfers – especially if it's overseas. This is the scammer payment method of choice and it should be avoided at all costs unless you know the other person extremely well.

Ready to bid or buy?

Here it is! You've read through the item page. You feel this may be the item you want. You've crossed your T's and dotted your I's. It is now time to bid!

For this item, the following is listed in the Ready to bid or buy section:

> Your maximum bid: US $ ____(Enter US $21.99 or more)

eBay is telling you that the minimum bid for this item is $21.99. You could go ahead and enter that value and the auction will begin. I suggest you complete this chapter first though. Coming up – bidding strategies. You won't want to miss it.

Bidding Strategies (nothing fancy)

When I hear the word strategy, I always think of long, drawn out and complicated plans. Not here. Instead, I think that it's important that you understand the two basic ways that you can bid on eBay: Straight and Proxy. Let's begin with Straight.

Straight Bidding

Straight bidding is fairly straightforward (pun intended). Here's an example of straight bidding in action.

> Bidder A: Locates item he wants to bid on. Reviews the item page and likes what he sees. Starting bid is set at $9.99. Down at the bottom of the page, in the Ready to bid or buy? section, the bidder enters his bid – $10.99.
>
> Bidder B: This second bidder locates this same item and bids as well at $11.99.
>
> Bidder A: Not to be outdone, Bidder A bids again at $12.99. After doing so, Bidder A, goes to sleep for the night.
>
> Bidder B: He bids again at 13.99.
>
> The auction closes that evening and Bidder B has won the auction.

The problem with straight bidding is that if you aren't chained to your computer, bids and auctions will slip right past you. Regardless of the fact that eBay will send you notifications when you've been outbid, if you aren't in front of your email program, you still won't get there in time.

Proxy Bidding

Absolutely free and built-in to eBay's bidding system, I would like to introduce you to proxy bidding. I know, I know – it sounds kind of scary. It's not. In fact, it is absolutely awesome and really easy to use. Here's an example of proxy bidding in action.

Bidder A: Locates item he wants to bid on. Reviews the item page and likes what he sees. Starting bid is set at $9.99. Down at the bottom of the page, in the Ready to bid or buy? section, the bidder enters his MAXIMUM bid – $18.99.

At $18.99, Bidder A is telling eBay that the maximum he will spend on this item is $18.99. The bid amount for this item will only go up by one dollar though. The current bid price is now $10.99.

Bidder B: This second bidder locates this same item and bids as well at $11.99. The bid amount increases to $12.99 but Bidder B is not the high bidder. Bidder A is. eBay has automatically played Bidder A's hand by counter bidding against Bidder B. Bidder A is still the highest bidder at $12.99.

Bidder B: Bidder B decides to bid again, this time at $14.99. The bid amount increases to $15.99 but Bidder B is still not the high bidder. Bidder A is. eBay has automatically played Bidder A's hand again by counter bidding against Bidder B. Bidder A is still the highest bidder at 15.99.

Bidder A: Bidder A is sitting in a restaurant having drinks with friends while all this is happening automatically with eBay at the steering wheel. His bids are in good hands.

Bidder B: Tired, but determined, Bidder B tries one more time by entering a bid of $17.99. The bid amount increases to

$18.99 but Bidder B is still not the high bidder. Bidder A is. eBay has automatically played Bidder A's hand again by counter bidding against Bidder B. Bidder A is still the highest bidder at $18.99.

Bidder B: Defeated, Bidder B decides to pack it in and does not place another bid.

Bidder A: Auction ends, and Bidder A wins the auction.

Proxy bidding is definitely the way to go. Set your maximum and put your feet up and let eBay do the rest.

Pssst. Here's a small bidding tip! Many people like bidding in nice, even increments. For example, most people will bid $10 or $85 or 105.50. Rarely do people bid strange uneven numbers like $11.43 or $84.67 or $105.51. Try it. You can sometimes outbid someone by 1 cent.

Win, Lose or Buy?

Now that we have a better idea of what the Item Page is telling us and have some solid bidding strategies under our belt, we are ready to win some auctions! Unfortunately though, you can't win them all. What are you to do if and when you lose an auction? Is there a protocol you should be following? What do you do when you win an auction? Enough of these questions. Let's get to the answers!

You've Won! Now What?

Alright! You've won your auction. What do you do next? There are only a couple of things you really need to do and again, eBay tries to make it as painless as possible.

Automatically, eBay will send you and the seller an email announcing the end of this auction and the verdict. You will be given all the information you need in order to complete the transaction. Here's how you should proceed:

- **Contact the Seller**. If you have all the information you need already, you may not need to contact the seller. I typically do anyway in order to confirm my numbers. The last thing you want to do is find out you had the shipping charges wrong. Ask (again) just to be sure.
- **Pay**. Be punctual. The way this works is that you pay, they send. It's a fairly simple process that always makes buyers feel a little antsy. How do you know if the seller is really going to send the item. You don't. This is where trust and honesty come into play. Hopefully you did some research into the seller before bidding on the item as well.
- **Wait**. Once you've sent payment to the seller, always ask that they confirm receipt. Some high almighty sellers will tell you not to bug them once you've sent payment. Those sellers I typically ignore and never deal with again. I like to know that my money has been sent and received. In addition, always ask (if it wasn't already noted in their listing) how soon they will ship and the estimated time of delivery to your address.
- **Receive**. Once you receive the item, it is your duty as a true eBayer to leave feedback for the seller. Be it a positive, neutral or negative experience, the rest of the eBay population wants to see it. Use the limited number of

characters wisely. You want to get your feeling across in a clear and concise way.

You've Lost! Now What?

You're bound to lose some so don't get your mouse into a knot. Use it as a learning experience and try to gain insight into why you lost in the first place. Here are some things to consider.

- **Can I contact the Seller?**. I wouldn't. Remember, you are not protected by eBay if you operate outside of its system. If you proceed to contact the seller after losing their auction, asking if they maybe have another item for sale, you are possibly opening yourself up to a scammer. Be careful. You are on your own.
- **Can I contact the Winner?**. I wouldn't. Again, you aren't protected if you deal outside of eBay.
- **Snipers**. Did you possibly lose to a sniper? Snipers wait until the last seconds of an auction to bid on an item. It's an age old bidding strategy that many feel hits way below the belt of good ethical bidding. The jury is still out on this one. Regardless, check the bid history for the item you lost out on. There, you can get a good idea of how the bidding went. If you were beat by a Sniper, I recommend you read the Sniping chapter in this book to get a better idea of how to fight back.
- **Proxy-less Bid**. Did you get caught away from your computer? Did you forget to bid high enough and let eBay do the bidding for you via proxy bidding. Now you've learned your lesson – right? Bid your maximum – always.
- **Sky High**. The most popular reason why people lose auctions though is because the price just went too high. That's an absolutely fair reason to pull out. Never fault yourself for that and always remember – that same item

probably just listed again from a different seller. Put this book down and get to bidding again! Good luck.

ScamMaster I.Q. Review

Knowledge is power in the war on scammers. Here is your chance to test your scam I.Q. against the master himself; ScamMan.

Questions

1. The ______ ______ area will not only tell you how long a member has been registered on eBay but also where they are located.

2. It is imperative that before you bid or buy an item from any seller, you click on their User ID or _________ _________ to visit their Feedback Forum.

3. True or False. Proxy bidding is a pay per use feature of eBay.

4. What is the advantage of bidding in non-even increments?

5. After you've won an item, why is it a good Idea to contact the seller?

Answers

1. Member Since. 2. Feedback Points. 3. False. 4. Most people use even increments so if you use non-even you can sometimes win by a few cents. 5. To confirm numbers.

eBay Scams Presents

THE ADVENTURES OF SCAMMAN

CHAPTER 6

Time to Sell

Time to Sell

The time is now. It is time to sell. Many people fear selling on eBay. They think it's too complicated or expensive. eBay must take a huge cut – right? Wrong. The cut eBay takes is actually quite nominal. You can really make a lot of money selling items on eBay if you're selling the right item, and your selling the right way.

In this chapter, we will learn how to:

- Prepare ourselves before we sell
- Understand the selling process on eBay
- Sell an item from start to finish

Prep Before We Sell

A wise man once said, "He who prepares, prepares to win!". When it comes to listing an item on eBay, this saying really applies. Preparation is key to any successful selling career.

You could just pick up your item, sit down at your computer and move through the selling steps one by one. I'm sure most people do it that way. Not me. I like to prepare before I sell. Let's take a look at some of things you should always do before you sell anything on eBay.

Check Completed Items

As you know, eBay gives you the ability to check into auctions that have already expired. If you're about to sell an item, why not check to see if similar items have sold in the past and at what price? It's easy to do and will bring you a whole wealth of information like:

- How much it sold for?
- How many people bid?
- How many auctions existed for this item?
- What did those listings look like?
- What was the starting bid price?

Using the following example, let's run through the steps required to check on completed items.

In this example, I am selling a DVD movie called Reawakening (not to be mistaken with the Robin Williams film, Awakenings). This is a small independent film made in Canada that had a limited release on DVD. Sure to be a collector's edition, I thought I would try my luck selling it on eBay.

1. From eBay homepage, I clicked on the Smart Search link located just below the What are you looking for? Search text box.

2. In the "Enter keyword or item number" text box, I typed the following keywords: Reawakening DVD.

3. I enabled the Completed Listing Only check box on the Find Items page.

4. I then clicked on Search.

Only four results were returned in the search results list. They looked something like this:

Reawakening - NEW DVD $9.99 – 4 - Oct-14 14:10

Reawakening - (Andrew Louis Smith) - New DVD
$9.74 – 2 - Oct-11 19:13

REAWAKENING HEATHER ARCHIBALD - NEW DVD
$10.75 – 5 - Oct-08 19:57

Reawakening (1997) DVD Archibald, Smith, Miller
$5.24 – 2 - Oct-02 20:37

What did this tell us? Well, every number listed following the price tells us the number of bids that item received. We have a range of 2 bids all the way to 5. The highest price fetched for this item was $10.75. Looking at each of the listings in detail, I was also able to come up with some good ideas as to how I planned on designing my ad.

At the very least, looking at the completed items let me know that there was an audience for this film and that people were willing to spend some money to buy it.

Research Your Item

Before you sell anything on eBay, really make sure you know your item inside and out. In order to list it properly, you have to include accurate information and also be able to respond to any questions that may come your way.

To gain a better understanding of the DVD I was selling, I searched on its title using Google. Several results were returned and I proceeded to read up on the film, the DVD specifications, behind the scenes information and the extra features. All of this information would come in really handy when I created my listing description.

Subject Matter Experts (SME)

Depending on what you are selling, you may want to speak with a SME before you hit the boards. If you are selling a computer system and you aren't a tech-head, I would really recommend speaking to someone who understands the system and would know how to price it. Websites can only get you so far when you are researching a more complicated item like a musical instrument, computer system or hi-fi stereo. Go to your local stores, join a club or visit a tradeshow – there are experts all around you willing to give their advice for free.

Are There Any Selling Now?

Is your item a high demand item? Are there hundreds for sale currently on eBay? Sometimes, just running a search for your item on eBay will give you an idea as to its demand at that moment. If there are hundreds of your item for sale, and no one is bidding – don't waste your time. On the other hand, if there are only a few selling, and there are bids coming in, you may be able to get into the game.

Organization is Key

I like to save the best tip for last. When you finally decide to take the plunge and sell items on eBay, it is very important that you stay organized. It can get really hectic when you have more than one item selling at the same time. Just imagine the following things all happening at the same time:

- Potential buyer asking a question
- Shipping an item to a buyer
- Listing an item

- Dealing with a refund

It's very easy to get inundated and the small details can slip through the cracks. The consequences of such disorganization can be grave – negative feedback. Here are some suggestions as to how you can stay organized when selling on eBay:

- Include following disclaimer in all emails/listings:

Please include Item Number in all communications.

This makes life a whole lot easier by allowing the seller to quickly reference the item in question.

- Create a folder system (both hard copy and soft)

On your computer, keep a record of everything you send out and receive. In addition, keep hard copies of all communications as back up, organized into a folder system.

- Customer Service #1

Setting the right priorities will really help you stay organized. Remember – you are in this business to serve your customer. I'm not going to bore you with the "Customer is always right" because we all know that's not true. What is true though is that you must make it a priority to respond to your customer's queries or your career selling on eBay will be very short-lived.

- Use My eBay

My eBay tracks all your eBay activity. When you're selling more than one item My eBay becomes your most important tool. Please refer to Chapter 7, My Very Own eBay for more information on this feature.

Getting Started

Feeling better now about selling? I thought you would. I feel great knowing we really prepared ourselves for this day. Item in hand, information all around me, we are ready to embark on our selling expedition. Let's begin by clicking on the Sell button on the eBay toolbar.

Using the previous example DVD, let's go through the necessary steps of listing this item on eBay.

Selling Format

From eBay's Sell page, click on the Start a New Listing button. Enter the world of Selling Formats. You have three choices to pick from and they are listed below:

- Sell item at online Auction. This auction format allows for both bidding and buy it now action.
- Sell at a Fixed Price. This auction format allows for set pricing only. No bidding.
- Advertise your Real Estate. This auction format is reserved for people advertising and selling real estate.

For this example, we will proceed by selecting the *Sell item at online Auction* option. My plan is to allow bidding but also offer a Buy It Now price.

Categories, Categories, Categories

If you recall from Chapter 4, The Art of the Search, we looked very closely at the category browse features available to buyers on eBay. Now it's your chance to assign a category to the item you are selling. Think about it for a minute. If someone chooses to category browse rather than search outright for your item, you want to make sure your item is assigned properly.

For the example of the Reawakening DVD, I went through the following steps:

1. After selecting the *Sell item at online Auction* option, I clicked on the Continue button.

2. On the *Sell Your Item: Select Category* page, I have several options to pick from.

The goal here is to select the most appropriate top-level category for your item. For this DVD, I think it's obvious which one I should pick: DVDs & Movies - DVDs, VHS tapes, laserdiscs, film, and other movie formats

3. I selected the DVDs & Movies option and scrolled down the page.

4. At the bottom of the page there is an additional option to choose a second category. Without getting into too much detail regarding fees, this little extra is not free. Keeping my hand on my wallet, I decided to pass and clicked on the Continue button.

5. On the following page, you are asked to select subcategories for your item. The following list of choices are presented based on my initial top-level DVDs & Movies selection.

- DVD
- Film
- Laserdisc
- VHS
- VHS Non-US (PAL)

- Other Formats
- Wholesale Lots

The choice is quite obvious. I went ahead and selected the DVD subcategory. This is the most likely place anyone would browse if they were looking for DVDs.

6. Again, you are asked if you want to include a second category. I pass on this second request and click on the Continue button.

7. On the following page entitled *Sell Your Item: Choose a Listing Option*, you are given the choice to either list with Pre-filled Item Information or list the standard way. Using the pre-filled option, eBay automatically fills your listing with Item Specifics information like movie descriptions, photos, reviews, actors, etc. All you have to do is enter a unique product identifier like a UPC code, title or director. This is a real time saver and I recommend it if you are selling something mainstream like a popular film or music CD. In this case, due to its limited release, this DVD did not show up in eBay's database of pre-filled listings. Instead, I went with the standard way of listing and clicked on the Continue button.

Title & Description

Here we are at the most exciting point in the selling process. Here's your chance to dust off your marketing degree and put your advertising skills to use. This section is all about promotion and making your listing accurate, informative and memorable. To put it in perspective, a poorly designed listing can crush a sale regardless of how popular or attractively priced your item is.

The Title

On the Sell *Your Item: Describe Your Item* page, you will be first asked to punch in a title. You have a limit of 55 characters so make sure that every letter counts. The following are some tips on creating effective titles:

Think like they do

When someone is searching for your item on eBay, what keywords do you think they would use? That is a very important question. If you can't answer it, I suggest you find someone who can. All of those keywords (if possible) should be included in your title.

Use All of your Characters

You have 55 characters to pick from. Use all of them. Even if you have some left over, make every effort to come up with secondary keywords that you could use. If you're at a loss, remember that you can always include words for the item's condition, model number or year of manufacture.

Don't Mislead

A popular "scam" tactic when creating titles is to include words that are completely unrelated to the item for sale in hopes of drawing in more buyers. The following is a great example of this misleading practice:

> Casio Hi-FI Stereo. Not Sony, Toshiba, Hitachi, RCA.

*)&#$&)%#

Never waste your time including punctuation, symbols, etc. in your item title. If you have the space for those symbols, you could put it to better use. Make the effort – its worth it. The following is an example of bad title wasting valuable characters on symbols and punctuation:

> !!!***Casio Hi-FI Stereo!!!Great Sounds***!!!

Use Acronyms (smartly)

There are several universally accepted acronyms that you can use which will greatly reduce the number of characters you need to use in your title. In most cases these acronyms describe the condition of the item. The following are examples of widely accepted acronyms used on eBay:

S/H	-	Shipping and Handling
NIB	-	New In Box
NIP	-	New in Package
NR	-	No Reserve
OOP	-	Out of Print
PC	-	Poor Condition
VF	-	Very Fine
VG	-	Very Good
VGC	-	Very Good Condition
WS	-	Widescreen

For the DVD I was selling, I decided to go with the following title:

> Reawakening DVD NIB NilSix Pictures Archibald Smith

Item Specifics

In the Item specifics section of this page, you can select from various drop-down menus the genre, sub-genre, condition, display format, rating and region code. This feature saves you the time of having to type out that information in your item description section. Here's what I went with for my DVD:

> **Genre:**
> Other
>
> **Sub-Genre**
> Blank
>
> **Condition**
> New
>
> **Display Format**
> Full Screen
>
> **Rating**
> NR
>
> **Region Code**
> Region 1: US, CA

Item Description

The item description is another very important part of your listing. Your item description section should include many of the following things (depending on your item):

- What is the benefit of your item? What is the value proposition?
- Item condition
- Features
- Specifications
- History of item
- Year and Make
- Special characteristics (i.e. signatures, stamps, editions, printings, etc.)
- Reviews (if applicable)

I've come across listings where the seller only included the name of the item and his price. That was it. I walked right past that listing and went on to the next. Many people (like me) do not have the time to contact sellers asking them all sorts of questions about their item. We expect a certain amount of base detail in a listing and when it's not there, we simply move on to the next.

eBay gives sellers the option of using straight text when creating their descriptions, using tools similar to your favorite word processor or the option to create your description using HTML. Make your decision based on what you're comfortable using. Personally, I find using the text version easier and faster for me. You can make your listings look great using eBay's built-in tools for formatting and themes.

Here's the content I created for my DVD's item description:

MINT CONDITION DVD – REAWAKENING – THE TRUTH DECEIVES

Collectors Edition – Limited Release DVD

This Region 1 DVD is in new condition and is available only in limited release. Sure to be a collector's edition, this DVD combines several genres including crime, drama and horror. Enjoy!

BONUS: If you win this auction – you'll also get a collector's edition Lobby Card from the film's premiere!

Film Description

One night, on a routine stakeout, detectives Nick Mitchell (Douglas James Miller) and Phil Lewis (Jerome Bourgault) witness an event so unbelievable that it leaves Phil dead and the other changed forever. Five years later, Nick is removed from active duty and suffering from guilt and depression hoping to solve the mysteries of that tragic night. Eventually, Nick starts unraveling a case that leads him to believe his partner isn't really dead after all. A unsettling look at the corrupt and lucrative black market antiquities trade, REAWAKENING is a tautly constructed policier-noir from local first-time feature director Andrew L. Smith, who also wrote, produced and edited the film. Shot entirely in and around Ottawa, the film is a dark, complex addition to an already warped and weird catalogue of local independent films. The film also stars

Heather Archibald, Bryan Farr, and the inimitable Phil Caracas, of Harry Knuckles fame.

- **Special Features**
- Director's Audio Commentary
- 45 Minute Making of Documentary
- Original Actor's Screen Tests
- Full Screen
- Region 1

Please e-mail me with questions BEFORE bidding. Payment by Paypal, cashier's check or money order are all accepted. I will ship within 2 days of receipt for these payment methods.

Pssst. If you're not a big fan of eBay's formatting features, you can type up and format your item description in your favorite word processor and then copy/paste the content into the item description box provided.

Pictures & Item Details

On the page that follows (Sell Your Item: Enter Pictures & Item Details), we are asked to start entering information regarding the item's price and auction duration. Let's take a look at each section, one by one:

- Start Price. This is the spot where you enter your item's opening bid amount. The lower your opening bid, the more action your item will typically see. Based on your research (See "Prep before We Sell" in this chapter), you should have a good idea as to how this item has sold in the past. You should also have a good indication as to what kind of starting prices were used and how successful those auctions ended up being. Use this research to select your opening bid price.

- Buy It Now Price. If you're willing to part with your item a at certain price, you can enter it here in the Buy It Now section. This allows buyers to purchase your item at a set price (you dictate) without having to enter any bidding process. There is an additional fee of 15 cents to the seller to include a Buy It Now price.

- Reserve Price. The minimum price the seller is willing to accept and below which an item will not be sold. This amount is confidential but potential buyers will see that a reserve price exists for that auction.

Pssst. A word of advice – unless you absolutely must, do not include a reserve price for your items. Many potential buyers will bypass any auction with a reserve because they feel they won't get the bargain they are looking for. Instead, raise your opening bid price – but not too high! That will scare off prospective buyers as well!

- Duration. You have the choice here of the following durations for your auction listings: 1 day, 3 day, 5 day, 7 day and 10 day. Many would think that the longer your item is listed, the better chance it sells. This can be true but it can also work against you. How your auctions are timed, in terms of start and end dates is actually more important sometimes. For example, an auction ending on a weekend, during non-sleep hours, has a better chance of finishing favorably than one that ends on a Monday night at 3AM. Plan ahead and definitely keep a clock and calendar handy.

Picture Mania

How and what kind of pictures you add to your listing can sometimes mean the difference between your item selling and not selling. It's that important. To really bring that point home, ask yourself the following simple questions:

1. Would you purchase something you couldn't see?

2. Would you purchase something you couldn't see from someone you didn't know?

3. Would you purchase something you couldn't see from someone you didn't know, over the Internet?

I think you get the picture (forgive the pun).

In this section of the selling process, eBay provides an upload picture service that makes displaying your pix a dream. Your first picture is free (thanks eBay!), while any others are 15 cents each. It's worth it to include as many pictures as you can - without breaking your bank of course. To add pictures to your listing, simply click on the Add Pictures button, locate the image on your hard drive and click Open. Its as easy as that.

For the Reawakening DVD that I'm selling, I took several pictures from different angles. I also took a photograph of the bonus item – an official lobby card from the film's premiere showing.

Pssst. I really recommend getting your hands on a digital camera if you plan on selling lots of items on eBay. They're really affordable and you wouldn't need anything fancy if it's main purpose were for online photos. Even a 1.3 megapixel camera would do the trick and still produce fantastic pictures you could upload for your eBay listings, email to friends or post on websites.

Of the four different picture options available, I selected the standard presentation - to save a little bit of cash. eBay gives you the option to present your buyers with Super Size Pictures, running slideshows and combination picture packs. Explore these different options and select what works for you, your item and budget.

Pssst. Always include photographs with your listing that YOU actually took rather than steal or borrowing images from other websites. Potential buyers will be more apt to believe you actually have the item your selling if they see that it's a real homemade picture rather than the manufacturer version.

Your Own Designer

If you're not an experienced web developer, eBay provides sellers with their very own listing designer. With over a hundred different templates to pick from, sellers can select and then apply different theme formatting to their listings. There are also four different listing layouts to pick from.

Figure 6.1 displays an example of how my listing will appear so far.

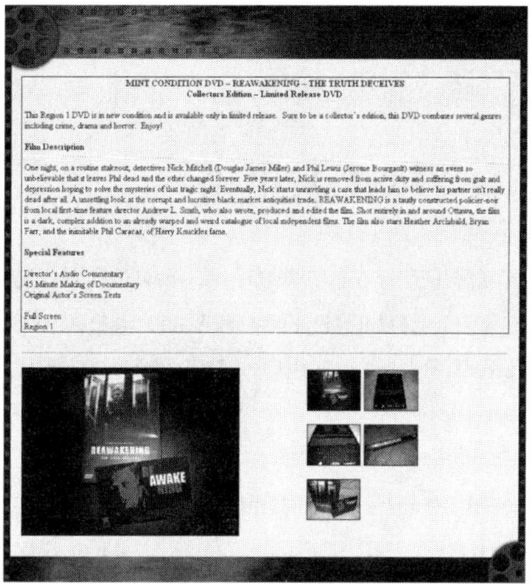

Figure 6.1 – My Listing So Far…

Increase Your Item's Visibility

eBay also offers several features (at an extra cost) that will make your item stand out from the rest. Depending on your item, some of these options will be worth the extra fee. The following makes up a list of those features available:

- Gallery options
- Bold
- Border
- Highlight
- Featured Plus!
- Home Page Featured
- Gift Services

Consult eBay's help files for more information and visual examples of each feature presented in this list.

For the item I'm selling, my budget wouldn't allow for these extra features. If you've got the money, some of these features can really make your item rise to the top.

Pay Me and Ship That Thing!

On the *Sell Your Item: Enter Payment & Shipping* page, you are asked to choose the payment methods you'll accept from buyers. You are also asked to enter the following information regarding your item:

- Ship-To Locations. This is where you tell your potential buyers where you are willing to ship your item. If you will only ship within North America, then you would list that here.

Pssst. If you plan on shipping worldwide, really make sure you research the country your shipping to. Get your shipping company to explain to you the risks, custom policies, legalities, etc. before you ship your item.

- Shipping Costs. eBay has excellent shipping costs features where you can enter a flat rate or actually have the costs calculated depending on the buyer's address.
- Refund Policy. Do you stand behind your item? This is a great way to show your customers that you really are a legitimate business. Knowing there's a refund policy allows members to bid with confidence.
- Payment Instructions. If there are any special payment instructions that you feel you need to include, enter them here.

Pssst. To avoid being labeled a scammer, keep your shipping costs front and center when creating your listings. Always be clear on what those costs are and never charge hidden handling fees unless it is absolutely necessary. In those cases, always let your bidders know by mentioning the additional fee in your listing. Do not surprise winning buyers with a handling fee after the auction has ended.

The following is an example of what you might include in this section:

> Please e-mail me with questions BEFORE bidding. Payment by Paypal, cashier's check or money order are all accepted. I will ship within 2 days of receipt for these payment methods.
>
> Personal Checks are also accepted but will be held for 2 weeks prior to item delivery.

Once you've entered all the necessary information on this page, click on the Continue button to enter the last and final stage of the selling process.

Final Step – Pay up!

For the final step of the selling process, you will come to the *Sell Your Item: Review & Submit Listing* page.

This is your last chance to review your listing before it goes live. If you see any issues or wish to change something, you always can by clicking the edit links after each section. Look very carefully.

Once you feel confident that the listing is perfect and suitable for framing, you have one last thing to review - the fees!

For my DVD, the costs are really low. To list my Reawakening DVD, the fees total up to $1.05. eBay takes a little more if I actually sell the item but again, the fees are nominal.

If you're ready – I'm ready! Go ahead and click on the Submit Listing button. You're listing is now live and ready for action. Good luck out there!

ScamMaster I.Q. Review

Knowledge is power in the war on scammers. Here is your chance to test your scam I.Q. against the master himself; ScamMan.

Questions

1. True or False. eBay gives you the ability to check into auctions that have already expired.

2. What is a SME?

3. How many characters can you use in your title when listing an item?

4. What does NIB stand for?

5. What are your options for the duration of your auction?

Answers

1. True. 2. Subject Matter Expert. 3. Fifty-five. 4. New in Box. 5. 1,3,5,7 or 10 days.

eBay Scams Presents

THE ADVENTURES OF

SCAMMAN

CHAPTER 7

My Very Own eBay

My Very Own eBay

Man oh man – I love this place! My eBay is the central hub of all your eBay activity. It tracks all your transactions, items your watching, favorite searches, sellers, lost auctions, winning auctions, preferences, blah, blah, blah. In other words – it does it all. My eBay allows you to manage your buying, selling and all other account activities.

In this chapter, we will learn about:

- My eBay's All Buying Pages
- My eBay's All Selling Pages
- My eBay's All Favorites Pages
- My eBay's My Account Pages

How Do I Get There?

To access the My eBay pages, click on the My eBay button on the main toolbar.

All Day Buying

When the My eBay page displays, you will series of links along the left side. Each link group is broken down into different categories. For the first category (All Buying), each link involves bidding or buying activities. They are, as follows:

Watch Me

Find an item you love but you're just not ready to bid just yet? Simply add it to your Watch List and let your My eBay page track it for you. You'll be alerted when that auction is about to end – giving you a chance to act!

Pssst. You can add items to your watch list by clicking on the Watch This Item link located in the top right corner of any item page you visit.

What is My Bidding, My Master…

If you've bid on an item, both that item and your bid amount will be tracked and managed from the bidding link on your My eBay page. The bid list displays very important information like time remaining in an auction, if you're winning or losing, photo links and up to date pricing.

I Won, I Won!

If you've bid on some items and actually won those auctions, eBay displays your wins on the Won page. It automatically totals your wins and the amount of money you've spent. You'll also find very helpful reminders to leave feedback for those sellers you purchased from.

I Didn't Win, I Didn't Win!

To get a good idea of what kind of losing track record you have on eBay, you can click on the Didn't Win link. There, you will see a running total of the number of losses you've had, as well as the money you saved. This list is a great way to stay on top of those items you may want to search for again at some point.

All Selling, All Day

Like the All Buying link, the All Selling link helps manage all your selling activities in one centralized location on the My eBay pages.

Schedule Me Please

When you go to list an item for sale on eBay, you are given the option of scheduling your go-live date to a date and time in the future. If you choose this option to future post your item, you can track its schedule using this link.

Sell Time

If you click on the Selling link, you will see all the items you are currently selling at that given moment in time. You will be provided with a running total as to how much you are currently making from those items and the number of items you've sold to date.

Going, Going, Gone and Sold

Think of the Sold link as being much like the Won list under All Buying. This is your list of successful sales complete with a running total of sales dollars and quantities sold.

Unsold

Like the Didn't Win link, the Unsold page will display all those items you weren't successful selling.

Pssst. Ask yourself why they didn't sell and maybe you can apply what you learned to future items you sell? Was your opening bid price too high? Did you set a reserve price and scare people off? Did you include photographs?

All Favorites, All the Time!

The All Favorites section of your My eBay page displays the three different types of Favorites you can save when using eBay. Each Favorite allows you quick access or shortcuts to selections you made on eBay. Here are some examples:

My Favorite Searches

If you recall, in Chapter 4 – The Art of the Search, we looked at saving Favorite Searches. This was a quick way for you to find a specific item, without having to set up the advanced search features each time. You can manage and edit your Favorite Searches from this section of your My eBay page.

My Favorite Sellers

If there are certain sellers you really trust or enjoy dealing with, you can set them up as Favorites and quickly access what they are selling. My eBay will manage this list of sellers and allow you to add more, quickly access their wares, or remove them.

My Favorite Categories

Are you a category browser like me? If you are, you can set up Favorite categories for quick access as well. Instead of having to drill down through several categories and subcategories to get to where you want to go, click on your Favorites and save yourself some time.

My Account Activity

In the My Account section of your My eBay page, you have complete control over the following information, subscriptions, preferences and accounts:

Now You're Getting Personal!

If you click on the Personal Information link, under the My Account section, eBay will display your user ID, Password, address details and financial information. You have the ability to make changes to these details whenever you please.

Subscribe to These!

From the Subscriptions link, eBay offers a whole slew of services on subscription that you can try and eventually purchase. You will find everything from Sales Reports to Selling Managers to eBay Picture Manager services. Take the time to read through the different subscriptions offered. It may be the edge you need to boost your sales!

eBay Preferences

This section is nothing to sneeze at – that's for sure. eBay does not skimp out when it comes to giving users the freedom to make their own choices when it comes to things like notifications, your sign-in, seller and My eBay preferences.

Pssst. Using the eBay Preferences page, you can set a certain view (like All Selling) to be your default page when you click on the My eBay button on the eBay Toolbar. To do this, simply scroll down the page to the My eBay Preferences section and make your changes.

Feedback

Using this link, you can quickly access all the feedback comments that have been left for you in your Feedback Forum. Your feedback score is displayed here as well as reminders for any feedback you still need to leave for other members.

Seller Account

All of your Seller account information is stored in this section. You must register a second time if you plan to sell on eBay. All the information you entered will be contained on this page where you are free to review and update if required.

PayPal Account

Like your Seller account information, you can access your registration information for your PayPal account from this section of the My Account pages. All the information you entered will be contained on this page where you are free to review and update if required.

ScamMaster I.Q. Review

Knowledge is power in the war on scammers. Here is your chance to test your scam I.Q. against the master himself; ScamMan.

Questions

1. You can add items to your watch list by clicking on the ______ ______ _______ link located in the top right corner of any item page you visit.

2. True or False. When you go to list an item for sale on eBay, you are given the option of scheduling your go-live date.

3. Name the three types of Favorites covered in the All Favorites section of My eBay.

4. True or False. The Feedback section of My eBay will remind you of the feedback you have yet to leave.

5. True or False. You can view your PayPal balance from the My eBay page.

Answers

1. Watch This Item. 2. True. 3. My Favorite Searches, Sellers and Categories. 4. True. 5. False.

eBay Scams Presents

THE ADVENTURES OF

SCAMMAN

CHAPTER 8

Gold Plated Shipping

Gold Plated Shipping

Here's a very popular scam that is so easy to defend against – it hurts. The problem is that people are lazy. Lazy people will always fall victim to the ScamMan and his cronies. Do your homework and follow some very simple rules and you can blow this scam right off eBay's website.

Scam Synopsis

By being purposely vague regarding shipping and handling costs, sellers will sometimes charge unsuspecting auction winners wildly padded prices to ship their item.

1. ScamMan creates a listing for an item for sale.

2a. In designing the listing, ScamMan intentionally does not include any shipping cost information. Figure 8.1 displays how ScamMan includes the following statement:

Please email with questions as items are final sale.

OR

2b. In designing the listing, ScamMan intentionally displays the shipping cost information in a very small font size, hidden within a mass of text. Figure 8.2 displays this very deceitful practice.

OR

SCAM FLOW

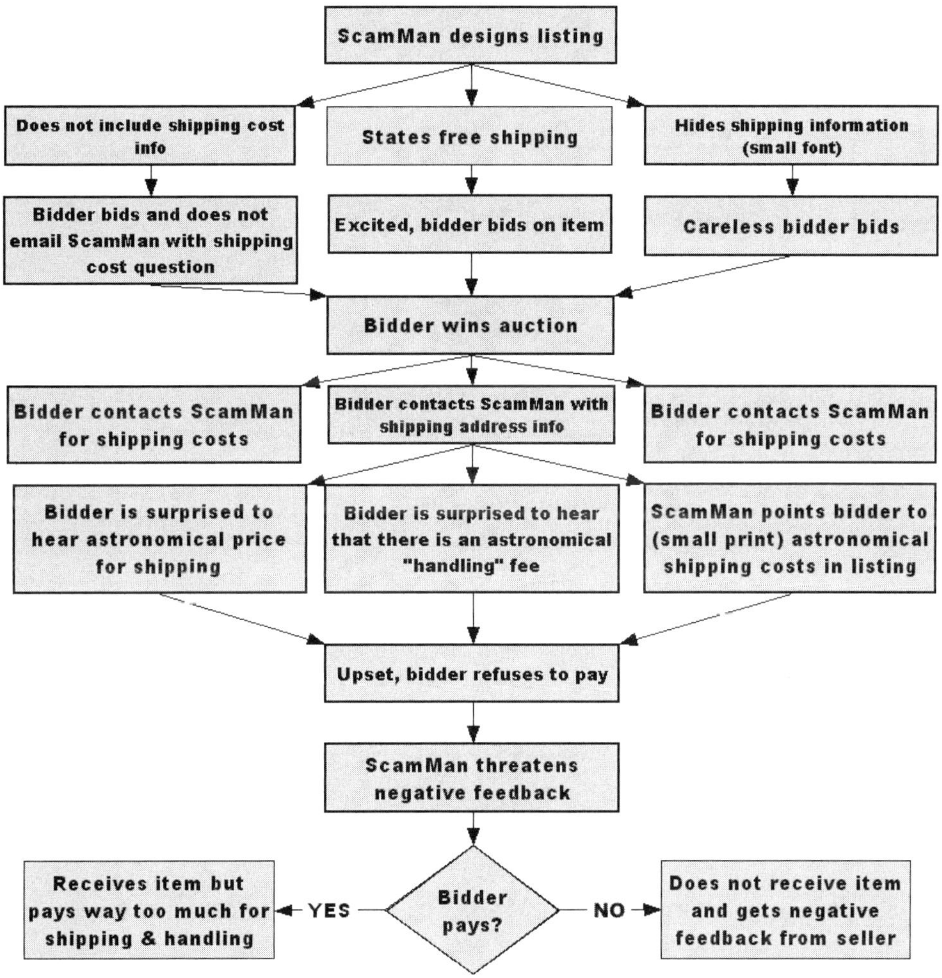

ScamMan designs listing
Does not include shipping cost info
States free shipping
Hides shipping information (small font)
Bidder bids and does not email ScamMan with shipping cost question
Excited, bidder bids on item
Careless bidder bids
Bidder wins auction
Bidder contacts ScamMan for shipping costs
Bidder contacts ScamMan with shipping address info
Bidder contacts ScamMan for shipping costs
Bidder is surprised to hear astronomical price for shipping
Bidder is surprised to hear that there is an astronomical "handling" fee
ScamMan points bidder to (small print) astronomical shipping costs in listing
Upset, bidder refuses to pay
ScamMan threatens negative feedback
Bidder pays?
YES
NO
Receives item but pays way too much for shipping & handling
Does not receive item and gets negative feedback from seller

2c. In designing the listing, ScamMan writes FREE SHIPPING in the item title and intentionally displays "handling" cost information in a very small font size, hidden within a mass of text – in the item description. Figure 8.3 displays an example of what ScamMan's listing looked like.

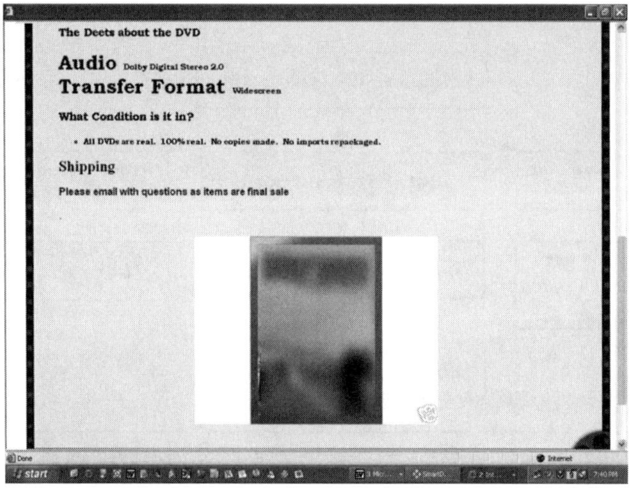

Figure 8.1 Vague shipping instructions can be very misleading.

3. Unsuspecting buyer bids and wins the auction for this item without emailing ScamMan with any questions regarding shipping costs.

4. eBay notifies both ScamMan (the seller) and buyer that this auction has ended with a sale. Emails are sent to both parties initiating the payment process.

5. The buyer emails ScamMan with his address asking how much shipping will cost.

6. ScamMan responds with a highly inflated price for shipping which includes all sorts of handling fees. These handling fees could include extra packaging, special padding, wrap and taping.

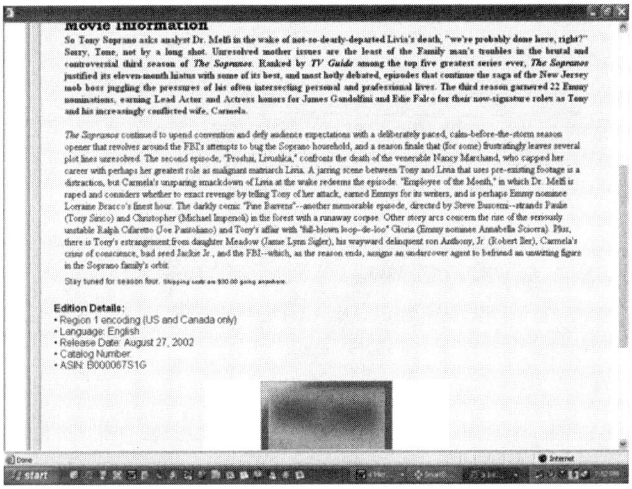

Figure 8.2 Shipping costs hidden within a mass of text.

7. Buyer is furious, and refuses to pay exorbitant shipping and handling charges.

8. ScamMan threatens to report buyer to eBay, on top of leaving negative feedback.

9. With his back up against the wall, the buyer agrees to pay the shipping and handling charge.

10. Upon receiving payment, ScamMan sends the item to the buyer.

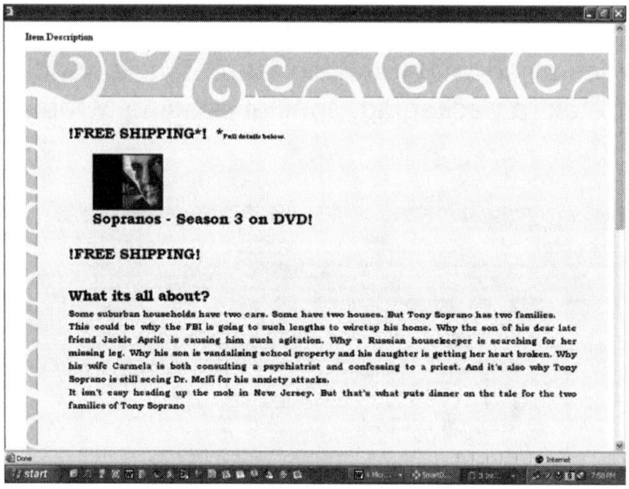

Figure 8.3 Shipping is free but handling costs aren't!

11. The package arrives at the buyer's house, shipped by regular mail, no special wrapping or packaging and the item is not properly secured in the box.

12. ScamMan does not post any feedback for buyer until he sees that positive feedback left for him.

13. Blackmailed, furious and tired, the buyer leaves ScamMan positive feedback so that his reputation on eBay is not tarnished by this brutal experience.

Best Defense

Try and understand the reason why people like ScamMan do what they do when it comes to outrageous shipping charges. The motive is actually quite simple - final eBay fees are calculated from the listing itself and its final value, not its shipping fees. By jacking up the shipping fees, sellers end up making more and actually paying eBay less.

Pssst. eBay does have a policy in place to ensure that sellers (like ScamMan) do not charge outrageous amounts for shipping. The term eBay uses to describe this practice is Fee Avoidance. eBay's listing policy states, in part the following:

"Listing Techniques that Circumvent eBay's fee structure.

Users may not use systems or techniques to circumvent eBay fees. Some examples include: Listings with low prices but unreasonably high shipping or handling costs"

How do you defend against this practice? Very easily. But – as I have mentioned before, if you're lazy (like me), you'll ignore these suggestions and keep on paying crazy shipping and handling fees. Take note, you may save yourself some money in the process.

Ask Questions

On every page, for any item selling on eBay, there's a handy dandy link called, Ask seller a question. By clicking on this link, you are transported to another page where you are free to ask the seller any question you want! Just imagine – you could actually ask the seller before you commit to anything just how much the shipping would be to your location. What a novel idea? How does that saying go again? Oh yeah - ask and you shall save. Remember to always keep on file all correspondence between you and the seller – especially as it relates to quoted shipping charges.

Shipping Calculator

Take responsibility. That's right – take responsibility. Regardless of the fact that you aren't the one actually shipping the item, you can still do some research on your own to get a better idea of how much it would cost to ship to your location. Using sites like, UPS and FedEX, you can calculate cost and time for shipments to and from specific locations. Ask the seller where they are shipping from. Ask them what shipper they plan on using. Estimate the weight of the item and you are off to the races.

Read It Carefully

There is no excuse for "not seeing" the shipping charges in an eBay item listing. Even if someone like ScamMan drops the point size on the font and hides it within a mass of text, that's not a valid excuse. Even eBay would have a problem siding with you if the seller did include the shipping costs and you just didn't see it. As a rule, always look for the following things when scanning a listing:

1. Shipping & Handling Costs

2. Where will this shipper to?

3. Condition of the item

4. Multiple Photos

5. The seller's feedback numbers and comments

This is a short list of must-sees for any listing. If by chance one or more of these things is missing from the listing, do one of two things: move on to the next one or ask the seller a question.

Specify Your Own Shipper

If you have your own account with a shipper like UPS or FedEx, always ask the seller ahead of time if he or she wouldn't mind using it. If the seller agrees, you can be sure they aren't marking up the shipping costs for your item.

Pssst. There are valid handling fees so you can't always raise a red flag anytime a shipping and handling fee seems high. Sellers will sometimes have to purchase materials in order to ship your item safely and securely. Those items may include: packing tape, special boxes, bubble wrap, labels, styrofoam, packing peanuts and padding.

ScamMaster I.Q. Review

Knowledge is power in the war on scammers. Here is your chance to test your scam I.Q. against the master himself; ScamMan.

Questions

1. What is the name of eBay's policy to ensure sellers don't charge outrageous amounts for shipping?

2. In his listing, ScamMan lists free shipping but deceptively includes a charge for ________ .

3. Name two of the five things you should look for when scanning a listing to see if this may be a case of gold plated shipping.

4. Are handling fees always a sign of a scammer?

5. What is one of the main motives for ScamMan to scam people on shipping?

Answers

1. Fee Avoidance. 2. Handling. 3. Shipping & Handling Costs, Where will this shipper to, condition of the item, multiple Photos, the seller's feedback numbers and comments. 4. There are valid handling fees so you can't always raise a red flag anytime a shipping and handling fee seems high. 5. By jacking up the shipping fees, sellers end up making more and actually paying eBay less.

eBay Scams Presents

THE ADVENTURES OF

SCAMMAN

CHAPTER 9

Misleading Titles & Descriptions

Misleading Titles & Descriptions

This is one of my all time favorites. On the scam-o-meter, this one rates pretty high. If it seems to good too be true – then it probably is. Remember that – especially as it relates to this scam. Read on my children, read on.

Scam Synopsis

Sellers will post an item on eBay and intentionally include a misleading item title and/or description. In most cases, the misrepresentation of the item greatly increases its desirability either by price, feature or manufacturer affiliation.

1. ScamMan creates a listing for an item for sale. In this example, he is selling a used Sony Trinitron TV valued at over $1000.

2. In creating his listing, ScamMan includes the following title:

Sony Trinitron TV. Fantastic Picture!

3. ScamMan includes starting bid price of $800.00.

4. His item description includes a detailed description of the item as well as photographs.

SCAM FLOW

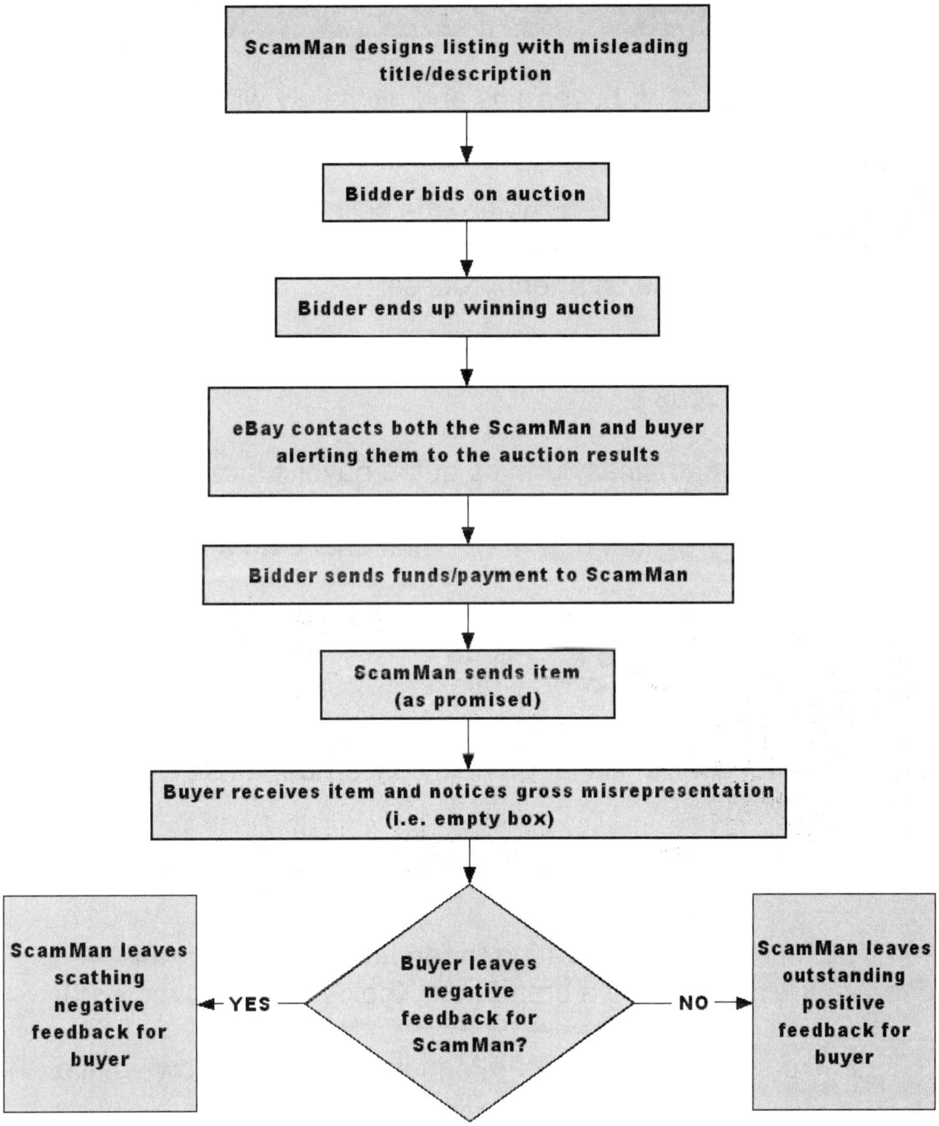
ScamMan designs listing with misleading title/description
Bidder bids on auction
Bidder ends up winning auction
eBay contacts both the ScamMan and buyer alerting them to the auction results
Bidder sends funds/payment to ScamMan
ScamMan sends item (as promised)
Buyer receives item and notices gross misrepresentation (i.e. empty box)
Buyer leaves negative feedback for ScamMan?
YES
ScamMan leaves scathing negative feedback for buyer
NO
ScamMan leaves outstanding positive feedback for buyer

Here's an excerpt from ScamMan's item description:

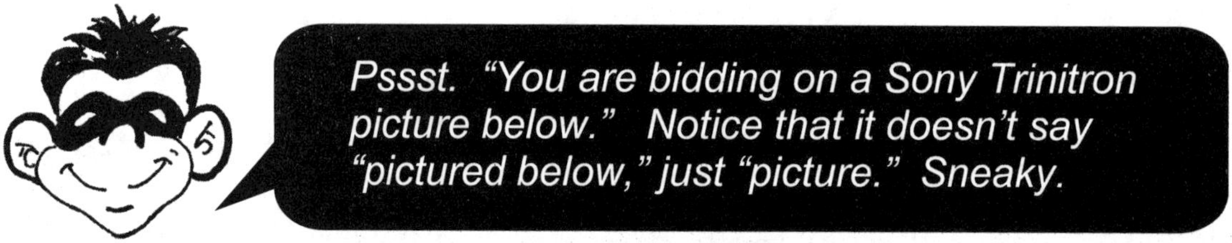

5. An unsuspecting buyer bids and ultimately wins the auction for this item.

6. eBay notifies both ScamMan (the seller) and buyer that this auction has ended with a sale. Emails are sent to both parties initiating the payment process.

7. Shipping costs are unusually low but the buyer does not ask any questions.

8. When the item finally arrives at the buyer's location, they are surprised to see that instead of an actual TV, the seller has sold him a picture of a Sony Trinitron TV (In a nice frame – to boot!).

9. Buyer complains to ScamMan.

10. ScamMan threatens to contact eBay and leave buyer negative feedback. As far as he's concerned, he's done nothing wrong.

Here's another variation on this popular scam!

1. ScamMan creates a listing for an item for sale. In this example, he is selling a brand new Xbox valued at over $200.

2. In creating his listing, ScamMan included the following title:

Xbox box for sale

3. ScamMan includes starting bid price of $9.99.

4. His item description includes a detailed description of the item as well as a photograph of the Xbox package.

5. A bidding war ensues and an unsuspecting buyer ultimately wins the auction for this item. These unsuspecting bidders assumed a typo in the item title and did not query the seller to be sure.

6. eBay notifies both ScamMan (the seller) and buyer that this auction has ended with a sale. Emails are sent to both parties initiating the payment process.

7. Shipping costs are unusually low but the buyer does not ask any questions.

8. When the item finally arrives at the buyer's location, he is surprised to see that instead of an actual Xbox, the seller has sold him a Xbox "empty" box.

9. Buyer complains to ScamMan.

10. ScamMan threatens to contact eBay and leave buyer negative feedback. As far as he's concerned, he's done nothing wrong.

I can't resist! Here's one more!

1. ScamMan creates a listing for an item for sale. In this example, he is selling a brand new Sony PlayStation II valued at over $200.

2. In creating his listing, ScamMan includes the following title:

PlayStation 2 Original Box And Receipt

3. ScamMan includes starting bid price of $9.99.

4. His item description includes a detailed description of the item as well as photographs of the item box and receipt.

5. A bidding war ensues and an unsuspecting buyer ultimately wins the auction for this item.

6. eBay notifies both ScamMan (the seller) and buyer that this auction has ended with a sale. Emails are sent to both parties initiating the payment process.

7. Shipping costs are unusually low but the buyer does not ask any questions.

8. When the item finally arrives at the buyer's location, he is surprised to see that instead of an actual PlayStation II, the seller has sold him a PlayStation "empty" box and receipt.

9. Buyer complains to ScamMan.

10. ScamMan threatens to contact eBay and leave buyer negative feedback. As far as he's concerned, he's done nothing wrong.

Best Defense

How do you defend yourself against this type of scam? Well, now that you know this practice exists – you're one step ahead – right? Here are some tips on the best ways to stay on top of this game.

Read Carefully

I can't say this one enough. There is no excuse for not reading an item listing in its entirety. Take your time and really analyze what you are reading. If there's even a shadow of a doubt as to the legitimacy of a title or description, either walk away or ask the seller a question. Remember – if it seems to good to be true – it probably is.

Ask the Seller

If there is any doubt in your mind, take the time to email the seller to be sure. Most scammers will typically ignore your email and not respond. Scam alarms should go off in your head as you run (not walk) to the next listing in your search results.

Google It

If a title seems a little questionable, try doing a search on Google (or any other similar search engine site). For example, if you were about to bid on an Xbox that seemed to have a shady title, search on Google using the following keywords: Xbox eBay scam. If scams exist for that specific item, Google will find them and you'll be one step ahead – and a little richer.

Starting Bids

Always be leery of extremely low opening bids for large ticket items. Low opening bids almost always create a bidding frenzy driving the price sky high as people spin out of control. Check the title and description just to be sure you aren't falling for this classic nugget of a scam.

Check Feedback

A seller's feedback forum will sometimes tell you if they've pulled this stunt before. Always check. Feedback is there for a reason and should always be consulted prior to making a bid. Here's an example of some feedback I found for a specific seller who was caught several times pulling this scam:

Stay away. Ships empty boxes. Absolute scam artist. No refund.

Its Not a Typo

Never assume anything. If you see a typo in an item's title or description and it's inclusion changes the item in a significant way (i.e. Xbox box), always query the seller using the Ask the Seller a Question link just to be sure.

ScamMaster I.Q. Review

Knowledge is power in the war on scammers. Here is your chance to test your scam I.Q. against the master himself; ScamMan.

Questions

1. What is the number one defence against misleading titles and descriptions?

2. Why is it important to ask the seller a question when you suspect a misleading description?

3. What web site can you visit in order to search to see if this item is commonly used as a scam?

4. Why should you suspect a low opening bid?

5. Why is it important to check a seller's feedback?

Answers

1. Read very carefully. 2. Scammers will typically not respond. 3. Google. 4. Low opening bids almost always create a bidding frenzy driving the price sky high as people spin out of control. 5. A seller's feedback forum will sometimes tell you if they've pulled this stunt before.

eBay Scams Presents

THE ADVENTURES OF

SCAMMAN

CHAPTER 10

Shilling

Schilling

Shillers beware! You're dirty methods are about to be exposed. Let's follow the exploits of ScamMan and his buddy Scummy as they go through the steps of shilling an unsuspecting eBay member. Unfortunately, this practice is as easy as it's going to sound. It's up to you – and only you - to protect yourself from the ScamMan's oily grasp.

Scam Synopsis

A slippery and in most cases illegal practice where sellers persuade friends or associates to bid on their own items in order to inflate the price.

1. ScamMan lists an item for sale on eBay.

2. Unassuming, innocent bidder bids on item.

3. No one else bids on this item. ScamMan grows impatient.

4. Auction end draws near.

5. ScamMan contacts friend/associate - Scummy.

6. Asks Scummy to bid on his item.

7. Scummy bids on ScamMan's item, slightly higher than the patsy bidder's amount.

8. Via proxy bidding, the innocent bidder's bid amount inches higher and is still the high bid.

SCAM FLOW

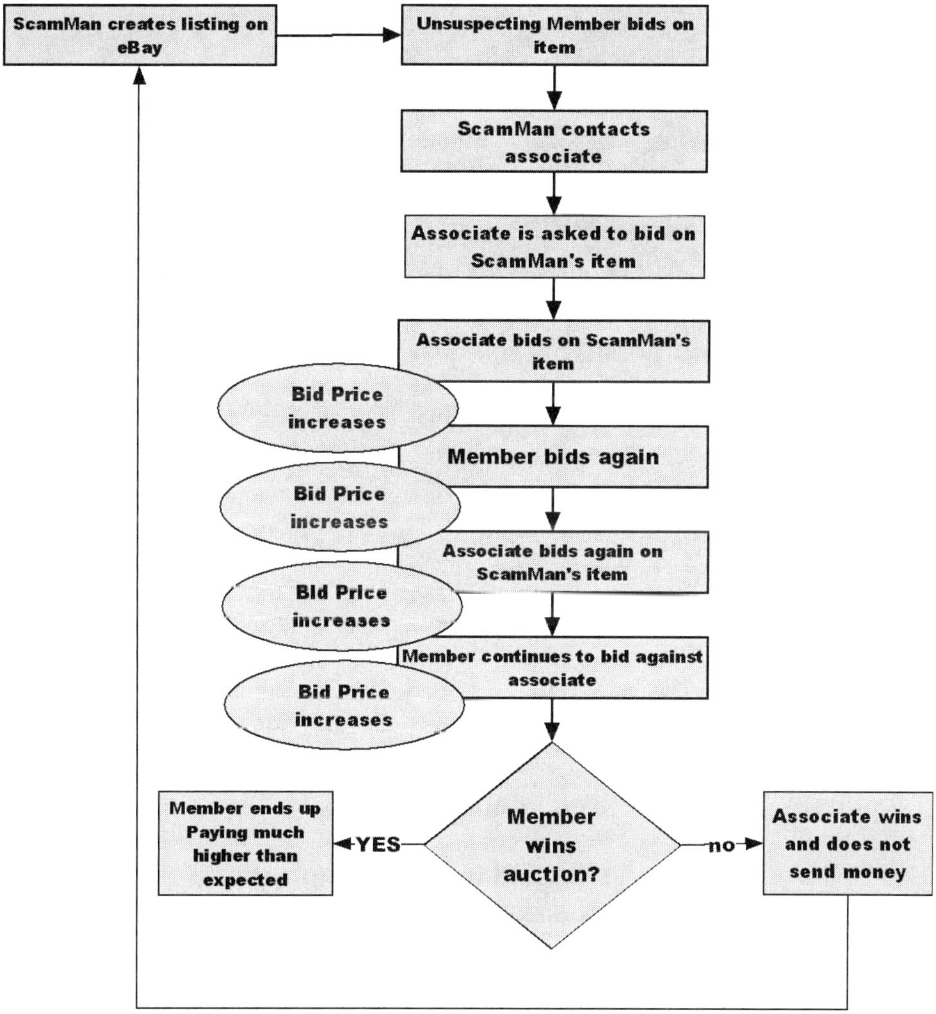
ScamMan creates listing on eBay
Unsuspecting Member bids on item
ScamMan contacts associate
Associate is asked to bid on ScamMan's item
Associate bids on ScamMan's item
Bid Price increases
Member bids again
Bid Price increases
Associate bids again on ScamMan's item
Bid Price increases
Member continues to bid against associate
Bid Price increases
Member wins auction?
YES
Member ends up Paying much higher than expected
no
Associate wins and does not send money

Pssst. In the early days, before Scummy became really scummy, he was reluctant to play ScamMan's game. His concern was, "What happens if I win?". ScamMan explained that even if he did win the auction, it wouldn't matter. All ScamMan would do is keep the item, pay eBay their nominal fee and no one's the wiser. In fact, ScamMan would go as far as asking friends like Scummy to leave him positive feedback even though no item changed hands. "No fuss – no muss", ScamMan would say with saliva dripping from his lips. Scummy would be off the hook with absolutely no obligation to do anything further. He would be scum-free, you could say.

9. Scummy bids again, bumping the patsy bidder's bid price up even higher.

10. The unsuspecting bidder is still the high bidder though.

11. Scummy continues to inch his bids up until Scummy himself becomes the high bidder.

12. Sweat begins to bead on ScamMan's head. Will the original bidder, bid again?

13. Victory – the unsuspecting bidder bids again to beat Scummy and ends up winning the auction.

The Shill wins again. It's tragic I tell you, simply tragic. Let's beat those boys by lining up a defense that works. Here are some things you can do to deter this from happening to you.

Best Defense

So now that you know what Schilling is all about, it's time to pick up that shield and defend yourself. *En Guarde!*

Know Your Limits

Know what you are willing to pay for an item and stick to it. Don't get caught up in auction hysteria. Check the web. How much is an item like this truly worth? Why pay more online, when you can walk into a store and buy it for less. Know your price and be a rock. Don't budge.

Bid Retractions

Keep an eye on auctions where bid retractions occur. This is typically a clear cut sign of a shill in action. Try and imagine. Someone like Scummy bids too high and ends up the high bidder for an item he's shilling on. Instead of following through, he simply retracts his bid, leaving the previous bidder as the high bidder again. Tricky, tricky, tricky.

Bid History

Check out the bid history for the item you are bidding on. Be wary of those bidders bidding against you with zero feedback points. Don't get me wrong, they may very well be legitimate – or not.

Private and Hidden

Keep your eyes open for those sellers who use hidden feedback or run private auctions. Those spell danger with a capital D. If the auction is private, that means that the bidder's identities are hidden, possibly hiding shillers playing in the trenches.

Safe Harbor

Contact eBay at safeharbour@ebay.com. If you feel like you are falling victim to a Shill, let eBay know. There are several spots you can go to ring the bell. The key here is to let them know. They can't stop what isn't reported. Lastly, understand that eBay has more visibility into what is happening on the backend of any auction that is running. Let them tell you what's what.

Check Their Other Auctions

If you feel someone is shilling you, check that bidder's other auctions. Take a look to see if that bidder is always bidding on certain seller's auctions. Then, if you do see a trend, are they consistently raising bid amounts without actually winning?

Outside the Walls

Avoid the post auction close sale. Sometimes, what you'll see happen is a seller will contact you after their auction has closed. They will claim that the true winner didn't pay and that you were next on the list of bids. Will you still purchase the item at your last bid amount – which was artificially inflated anyway. Don't do it! Make it a rule to never deal outside of eBay. Do so at your own risk because eBay provides no protection for members who stray.

Too Much Love Between Friends

Always check a bidder's feedback forum as well. What you're looking for here is a suspicious amount of positive feedback back and forth between the same seller and bidder. This can sometimes mean a seller and bidder are in cahoots and are practicing the shill.

ScamMaster I.Q. Review

Knowledge is power in the war on scammers. Here is your chance to test your scam I.Q. against the master himself; ScamMan.

Questions

1. What is Shilling?

2. Why is it important to find out the market price for the item you are bidding on?

3. A _______ ________ is typically a clear cut sign of a shill in action.

4. What is the name of the site you can visit if you feel you have been a victim of a shill?

5. True or False. You are protected by eBay for items that were listed but you end up purchasing privately, outside of eBay.

Answers

1. It is where sellers persuade friends or associates to bid on their own items in order to inflate the price. 2. So you avoid getting caught up in auction hysteria. 3. Bid Retraction. 4. Safe Harbor. 5. False.

eBay Scams Presents

THE ADVENTURES OF

SCAMMAN

CHAPTER 11

Phishing

Phishing

Pronounced "fishing", this prize winning scam is currently in the news and getting more and more popular – with scammers. Many say that Phishing has surpassed Spamming as the biggest pain in the butt on the web today. My goal is to make this scam even more popular but with a different audience – all of you! The more you know, the less likely you'll be duped when mysterious emails from eBay begin appearing in your inbox. Enough of this building suspense – read on and learn my friends.

Scam Synopsis

Scammers will send an email to an eBay member falsely claiming to be an eBay representative. The scammer's goal is to sucker the member into revealing their private information (i.e. passwords, credit card numbers, etc.) which will ultimately be used for identity theft.

1. ScamMan creates "look-alike" eBay website.

2a. ScamMan purchases database of stolen eBay member email addresses.

or

2b. ScamMan steals member's email addresses himself using the "Ask the seller a question" or "Contact a Member" feature on eBay.

3. With these addresses in hand, ScamMan designs a fraudulent email masquerading as an eBay representative.

SCAM FLOW

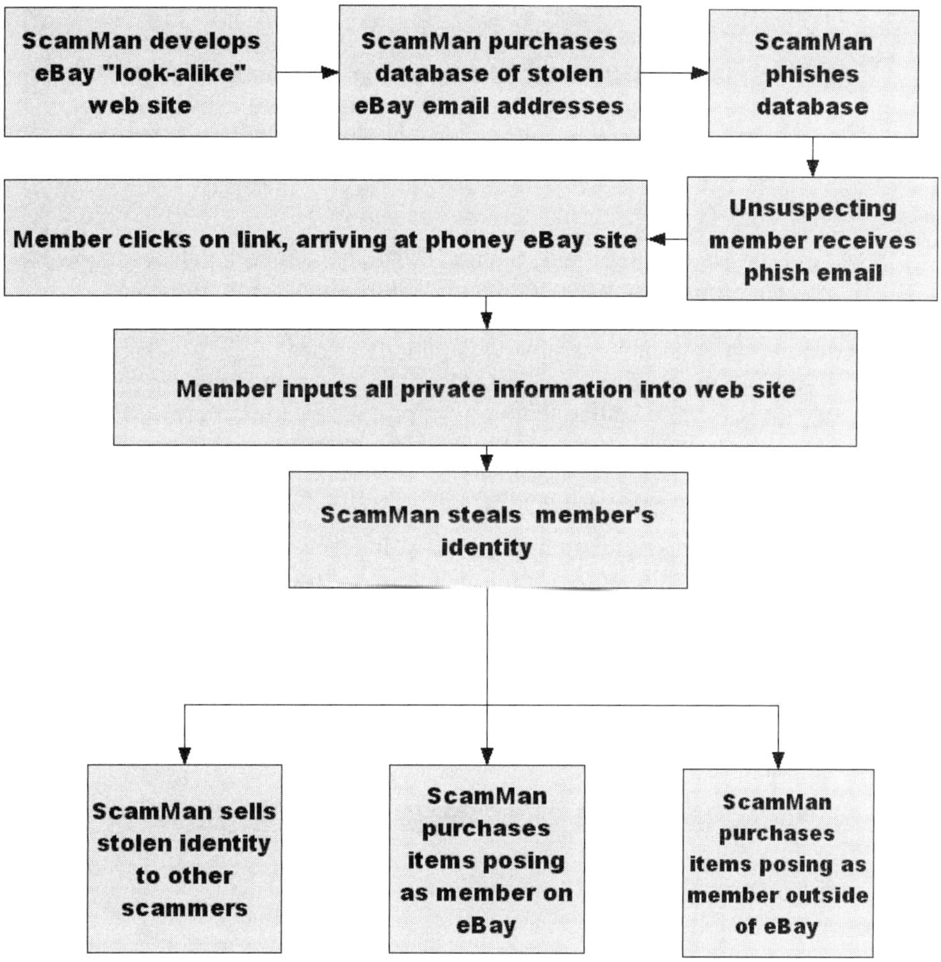
ScamMan develops eBay "look-alike" web site
ScamMan purchases database of stolen eBay email addresses
ScamMan phishes database
Unsuspecting member receives phish email
Member clicks on link, arriving at phoney eBay site
Member inputs all private information into web site
ScamMan steals member's identity
ScamMan sells stolen identity to other scammers
ScamMan purchases items posing as member on eBay
ScamMan purchases items posing as member outside of eBay

The following are two examples of popular spoof or phishing emails that have circulated the web. These emails will always contain a link to an eBay rip-off website or pop-up form where the unsuspecting person is encouraged to enter their personal information.

Email Example #1

Dear eBay member,

We have reasons to think that there are some problems with your eBay account. It is possible that these problems may cause your account to be temporarily suspended. Please login to your account by clicking here and check if all your personal information are right.

As per the User Agreement, Section 9, we may immediately issue a warning, temporarily suspend, indefinitely suspend or terminate your membership and refuse to provide our services to you if we believe that your actions may cause financial loss or legal liability for you, our users or us. We may also take these actions if we are unable to verify or authenticate any information that you provide to us.

Good luck trading on eBay!

Regards, Safeharbor Department eBay, Inc .
Do not reply to this e-mail

As outlined in our User Agreement, eBay will periodically send you information about site changes and enhancements. Visit our Privacy Policy and User Agreement if you have any questions. Copyright © 1995-2003 eBay Inc. All Rights Reserved.

Email Example #2

Dear eBay member,

As part of our continuing commitment to protect your account and to reduce the instance of fraud on our website, we are undertaking a period review of our member accounts. You are requested to visit our site by following the link given below. Please fill in the required information.

This is required for us to continue to offer you a safe and risk free environment to send and receive money online, and maintain the eBay Experience.

Thank you

Accounts Management

As outlined in our User Agreement, eBay will periodically send you information about site changes and enhancements. Visit our Privacy Policy and User Agreement if you have any questions. Copyright © 1995-2003 eBay Inc. All Rights Reserved.

Designated trademarks and brands are the property of their respective owners. Use of this Web site constitutes acceptance of the eBay User Agreement and Privacy Policy . Copyright © 1995-2003 eBay Inc. All Rights Reserved.

4. Using the stolen email addresses, ScamMan spams them with this fraudulent email.

5. Unsuspecting members receive this email and are immediately concerned. In the body of the email (seemingly coming from eBay), it states that their accounts will be suspended if they do not comply.

6. Confused and scared, many members click on the link within the email and are transported to a very convincing eBay "look-alike" site.

7. On this site, they are asked to sign-in (revealing their User IDs and passwords) and then proceed to enter their credit card information.

8. Once completed, ScamMan and his cronies collect this valuable and private information.

9. ScamMan and group must then decide what they want to do with the information. They have two choices:

- Sell it. There is a huge market for eBay member identities and ScamMan can make a lot of money selling them to underground buyers. Once successfully sold, member's identities are in effect hijacked and purchases are made both in and outside of eBay.
- Use it. Once an unsuspecting member submits their private information, ScamMan can hijack that user's account on eBay, and go on a buying spree. Keep in mind what we are talking about – credit card information, name, passwords and User IDs. You really wouldn't need anything else.

10. After submitting all their personal information, the member is redirected to the genuine eBay web site.

Pssst. Also known as brand spoofing or carding, phishing is a variation on the word "fishing". Most fish either ignore or take the bait. This is exactly what phishers expect eBay members to do – when they send their fraudulent emails.

11. As the days pass, hijacked member begins to notice strange transactions appearing on their credit card bills. They may also notice that their sign-in name and password no longer work on eBay.

12. They immediately contact eBay only to find out that the email and website were fraudulent – not coming from eBay's servers.

13. The victimized eBay member is now forced to go through the tedious process of retrieving their lost account and funds.

Best Defense

There are several things you can do to keep you and your family safe from phishers. Compared to spamming, phishing is a lot more dangerous and can do some real serious harm to your pocket book.

Do not respond

Never, and I mean never, respond to requests for personal/private information via email. Professional and responsible organizations will no longer request information this way. If you have any doubts at all, contact the organization making the request in order to verify first.

Do not click

When you receive emails that contain links and you are being asked to click it – don't! To ensure the site you are visiting is real, simply type the web address into your browser rather than clicking the link provided. For example, if an email asks you to visit eBay by clicking on a link, instead – type into your browser's address bar.

Check the Greeting

Keep your eyes open for questionable salutations. Many phishing emails start with a very generic greeting like, "Hello Friend" or "Welcome Member", rather than personally addressing you by name. Be leery. Be very leery.

Check the Spelling

Why can't scammers spell? Who knows but I can tell you that in a lot of cases, these spoof emails and websites are riddled with errors. If you see any, assume it phony and move on.

Encryption

Before you enter any information into a website, always check to ensure that the site is encrypted. In Internet Explorer, this is represented by a yellow lock that appears in the status bar, as shown in the figure below. This tells you that any information you do enter will be sent to their website using encryption methods.

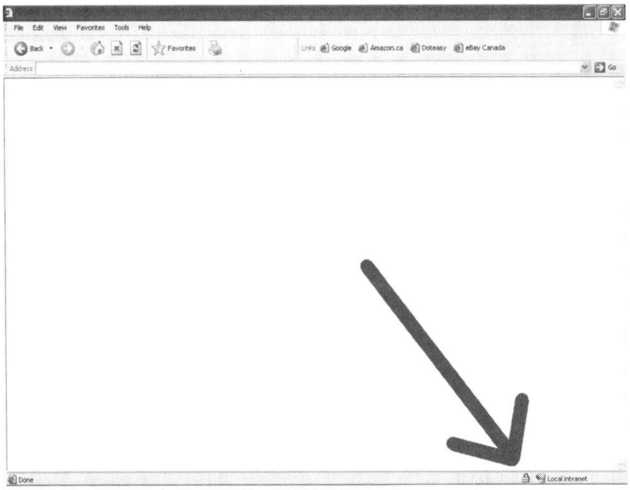

Encryption yellow lock

*Pssst. As a general rule, alway look at the wesite's URL or web address. If the address begins with http**s**, we know that the **s** stands for secure. Although this is ot a foolproof indicator of legitimacy, it's definately a good sign.*

This will keep your information safe and secure as it makes its way to the intended recipient.

Go ahead and double click the yellow lock in the status bar. A Certificate dialog will open. The name next to the Issue to should match the website you think you're on. If for whatever reason the name does not match, you may be on a phony site. Run don't walk and by all means, do not enter any information into this site.

Stay on top of your finances

Make it a habit to always review your finances especially as it relates to your credit and debit cards. Strange or unusual transaction behavior, if detected early enough can be resolved with your bank or card company quite promptly.

Lost and Found?

Do you really believe that companies like eBay and PayPal would actually lose your account information? I think not. Any email you receive that claims you need to update your account is most likely spoofing you. To be certain, type the website's actual URL into your browser and do it there.

Get the Toolbar

Did you know that eBay offers a freely downloadable toolbar that is intended to help people protect themselves against malicious phishers.

It's called the Account Guard and it has three major features:

Site Indicator

This feature is just too cool. The Site Indicator turns green if you are on a safe and secure eBay or PayPal web site; red if you are on a potentially phony web site; and grey when you are on a site that isn't eBay or PayPal.

eBay Password Protection

eBay will warn you when you're entering your eBay password into an unsafe site – even if it looks like it's really eBay or PayPal.

Report a Spoof Site

In a quick and handy location on the toolbar, if you feel you've found a spoofed or phony site, report the spoof site to eBay using this feature. Once eBay confirms it is indeed a fraudulent site, all eBay Toolbar users will benefit from having the most current information automatically uploaded to their toolbar.

Pssst. Careful! Scammers are getting trickier and trickier each day. Now, some scammers have worked it so that the web screen where you enter your personal information is a pop-up that lies on top of the real eBay page. In other words, what you are seeing is the fraudulent form on top of the real thing. Don't be fooled.

Be Leery of Attachments

Avoid opening attachments that are sent your way via email. There have been reported cases of email attachments containing something called Trojan Horses. These are files that are secretly downloaded to your computer to spy on you. These Trojans scan your system for personal and private information and send if off to the scammer in hiding.

Virus Checkers

Come on! Keep your virus checker up to date. It's so easy. Depending on which one you are using, it probably does it automatically. Virus checkers will keep offending files from being secretly downloaded and installed to your computer. Virus checkers that come with firewalls are also a great idea. Firewalls will keep you invisible to the outside world diminishing your chances of getting hit by the phish.

Uttering Threats

You'll also notice that many of the fraudulent emails coming your way will be in one way or another threatening to shut you down. Like a James Bond movie, there's always some sort of time limit before bombs go off. Don't buy it. This is a spoofer coming after you on the phish tip. You're informed. Don't be fooled.

ScamMaster I.Q. Review

Knowledge is power in the war on scammers. Here is your chance to test your scam I.Q. against the master himself; ScamMan.

Questions

1. What is the Scammer's goal when Phishing?

2. True or False. You should respond to the e-mails you receive asking to be taken off the list.

3. What is another name for Phishing?

4. How can you tell if a web site is encrypted in Internet Explorer?

5. What is eBay's password protection policy?

Answers

1. The scammer's goal is to sucker the member into revealing their private information. 2. False. 3. Spoofing or Carding. 4. A yellow lock appears in the status bar. 5. eBay will warn you when you're entering your eBay password into an unsafe site.

eBay Scams Presents

THE ADVENTURES OF

SCAMMAN

CHAPTER 12

Pyramid Scams

Pyramid Scams

Remember those pyramid schemes from back in the day? Well, they haven't gone away. Now, they've infiltrated eBay and fooled many a person out of their hard earned cash. They haven't changed much except now they're online, dangerously attractive and covertly camouflaged. Read up on this topic and avoid being duped by those scamming pryamiders who infest our online neighborhood.

Scam Synopsis

eBay members bid for an Internet link to an unspecified list of wholesalers, who are selling such wares as Apple iPods, TVs and stereos — at huge discounts. In reality though, once you win the bid, pay the seller and visit the website, you are told that you must pay another fee to be entered on to a list. The more people like you, who visit this site and pay the entry fee, the higher your name will float up the list – closer to the ultimate prize – your seemingly free item (i.e. iPod, TV, etc.).

1. ScamMan designs listing for free items as shown in Figure 12.1.

2. Curious bidder comes across listing and bids on these free items (via a web link).

3. Bidder ends up winning auction and paying ScamMan the winning bid amount.

4. As promised, ScamMan sends winning buyer the email with the web link included.

SCAM FLOW

ScamMan designs listing for Pyramid Scheme (selling a web link/URL) for free Apple iPOD

↓

Naïve bidder bids on item (web link)

↓

Bidder wins auction and pays ScamMan

↓

ScamMan sends winning bidder web link by email

↓

Buyer clicks on web link only to see that they now need to purchase something BEFORE they are entered on a list - for their "Free item"

↓

The buyer sits and waits indefinitely for his "free" item to be shipped (based on his/her position on this "list")

↓

Buyer is encouraged to recruit others to increase his position on the list

↓

Typically pyramid schemes run out of recruits and the scheme collapses

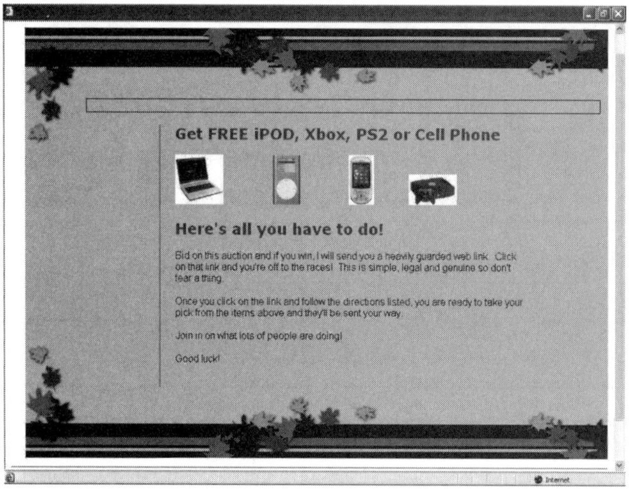

Figure 12.1 Listing free item – pyramid scheme.

Pssst. As you can see from this listing, ScamMan is not actually selling any "free" items. He's really selling this bidder an email. This email will contain a web link to a wholesaler that does sell iPods, PS2, cell phones – that can be "free", if certain conditions are met.

5. Buyer receives email and clicks on link, excited at the thought of getting his free items (i.e. iPod, cell phone, laptop)

6. Upon visiting this website, the buyer is upset to see that they now have to purchase something from this site BEFORE they can receive their "free" item.

7. The buyer ends up purchasing a low cost ($50.00) e-book from this site.

8. The buyer is informed that their name will now be added to a waiting list. As new recruits are brought in to this scheme, the buyer's name will climb higher on the list. Eventually, the buyer's name will hit the top and a free iPod (or other "free" item) will be shipped out to them.

9. The website encourages the buyer to recruit more people to their site. This will really speed things up and ensure the buyer gets their "free" iPod faster. The website even goes further to suggest different ways that the buyer could proactively seek out new people to join in. One of the suggestions is to create a listing on eBay.

10. Duped, the buyer goes back on to eBay and posts their own listing (similar to the one ScamMan created). There, they set the trap for other unsuspecting members and the vicious scam goes full circle.

Pssst. Pyramid/matrix schemes like this are so common on eBay that many buyers erroneously think their popularity is a sign of legitimacy.

How Popular is this Scam?

To see just how rampant this scam is on eBay, try the following:

1. Type www.ebay. com in your browser's address bar.

2. Click on the Smart Search link, located just below the What are you looking for? Search box. The Search: Find Items page will appear.

3. In the Enter keyword or item number search box, type iPod.

4. Click on the Sort By drop down menu.

5. Select the Price: Lowest First option.

6. Click on the Search button.

At the time I was writing this book, I ran out of fingers, toes and hair counting the number of matrix/pyramid iPod listings that polluted my screen. Go ahead, give it a try.

Best Defense

Unfortunately – once you're taken – you're taken. There are some things you can do after the fact but the bottom line is – you knew what you were getting into by buying a link to an outside site. eBay clearly states that any auctions listing items for sale OUTSIDE of eBay are against eBay's Terms of Service (TOS) policy. Any auctions selling web links or strictly information-only pages are clearly in breach.

Report to Matrixwatch.org

A website exists where a group of eBay watchdogs have banded together fighting this scam. You can report any suspicious auctions to the Matrixwatch.org by visiting their website at www.matrixwatch.org. The Watchdogs on this site will report the auction to eBay and add it to their database of matrix/pyramid auctions.

Report to eBay

If you prefer to go right to the source, you can contact eBay directly and lodge your complaint against these pyramid runners. Visit and send eBay an email with the item number. They'll do the rest. The following is an excerpt from eBay's listing policy. According to this page, eBay will look into the following actions based on what they find:

Disciplinary action may result in the indefinite suspension of a user's account, a temporary suspension, or a formal warning. eBay will consider the circumstances of an alleged offense and the user's trading records before taking action.

Things to Watch Out For

If you're not sure if a site is legitimate or not, the following things are typically red flags to avoid:

1. Seller is not really selling anything tangible.

2. Seller is selling a web link to other information.

3. Seller is promising free or astronomically low prices on any of the following items:

- iPods
- Plasma TVs
- Cell Phones
- Sony Laptops
- Computer Systems
- DVD Players
- Stereo Packages
- PlayStations
- Xbox

Typically, whatever is currently hot is fair game to these matrix schemers.

4. Seller is only allowing for "pre-approved bidders". When you come to their listing, you won't be able to freely bid like other listings. Instead, you must contact the seller first to be "pre-approved". This is their way of saying that they want to "speak" to you first. Their intention is most likely to convince you to go to a website and join the matrix/pyramid scheme.

5. Seller is selling a low-cost item, like an e-book which will in turn provide you with another more desirable item.

ScamMaster I.Q. Review

Knowledge is power in the war on scammers. Here is your chance to test your scam I.Q. against the master himself; ScamMan.

Questions

1. How is ScamMan making money off of the pyramid scheme?

2. What is another name for the Pyramid Scam?

3. What is the watchdog web site that helps protect people against pyramids?

4. True or False. eBay states that any auctions listing items for sale outside of eBay are against eBay's Terms of Service policy.

5. True or False. If a seller is selling a web link to other information, it's usually a good sign of a pyramid.

Answers

1. Entry fees. 2. Matrix. 3. Matrixwatch.org 4. True. 5. True.

eBay Scams Presents

THE ADVENTURES OF

SCAMMAN

CHAPTER 13

Sniping

Sniping

Sniping eh? Sounds dangerous. Let's put it this way – it's very popular and many members don't consider it a scam at all. How do you defend against a non-scam that actually feels like a scam on eBay? Read on my friends, read on.

Scam Synopsis

Bidder will place a winning bid seconds before an auction ends. By bidding at the last second, competing bidders are not given the chance to counter bid on an auction.

1. Sniper modifies his or her browser settings to disable graphics. Here's how he does it in Internet Explorer 6.0.

- Open Internet Explorer.
- Click on the Tools menu.
- Click on Internet Options. The Internet Options box will open.
- Click on the Advanced tab.
- Locate the Multimedia header in the scroll list of options.
- Remove the checkmark from within the check box next to the option Show Pictures.
- Click on OK to exit and save this browser option modification.

Pssst. The key here is to reduce the amount of time it takes for a sniper's screen to redraw or refresh when the refresh button in their browser is used. By stopping graphics or photographs from displaying in a browser window, web pages will appear much quicker – for the purpose of sniping! Keep reading, readers, the worst is yet to come!

SCAM FLOW

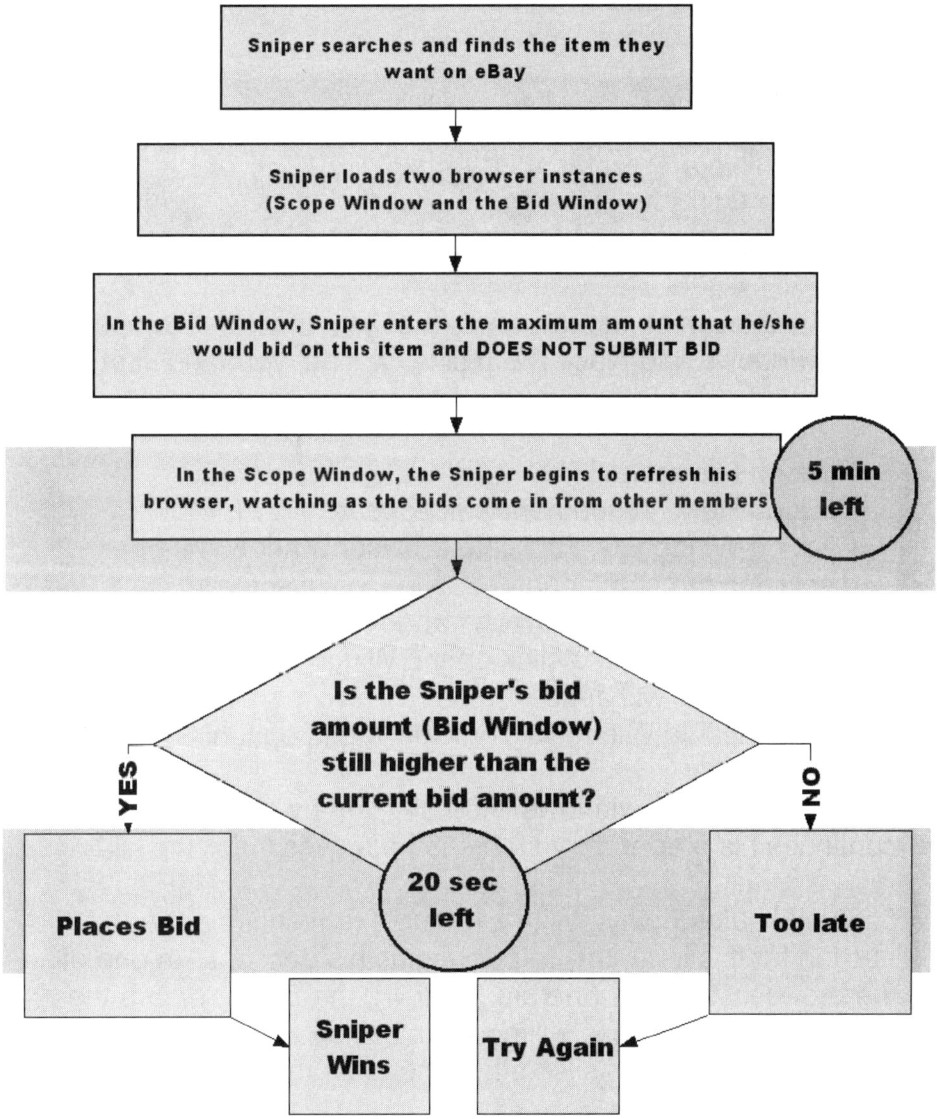
Sniper searches and finds the item they want on eBay
Sniper loads two browser instances (Scope Window and the Bid Window)
In the Bid Window, Sniper enters the maximum amount that he/she would bid on this item and DOES NOT SUBMIT BID
In the Scope Window, the Sniper begins to refresh his browser, watching as the bids come in from other members
5 min left
Is the Sniper's bid amount (Bid Window) still higher than the current bid amount?
YES
NO
Places Bid
20 sec left
Too late
Sniper Wins
Try Again

2. Sign-in to eBay. The last thing any sniper would want to see is the eBay sign-in page when they're trying to final second snipe an auction.

3. Locate the prey. In this case, the prey is the item the sniper is attempting to snipe on. Once a sniper locates the snipe target, he sits, seemingly lurking, and plans his attack.

Pssst. Snipers are crafty and resourceful. We are about to expose how snipers snipe in order to better understand this crazed and fast moving tactic.

4. Open two browser windows with that item in view. To open two browser windows and place them side by side, you must first do the following:

- Click on File menu.
- Click on New. A submenu will appear.
- Click on Window. A duplicate browser window will open displaying the same content as the initial screen.
- With only these two browser windows open on your Windows desktop, right mouse click on the Windows task bar. A list of menu options will appear.
- Select the Tile Windows Vertically menu option.

With both browser windows lined up, side by side, the sniper continues his preparatory steps as he moves in for the kill.

5. Five Minutes Away. With 5 minutes remaining in the auction for this item, the sniper begins his descent. In one of the browser windows (the bid window), the Sniper enters the highest bid he or she is willing to pay. You only get one chance to snipe so this isn't the time to be frugal. Bid as

much as you can and are willing to spend. You will not have time for another crack if your bid price is too low.

Pssst. Please note that I didn't say, the Sniper enters and submits the highest bid he or she is willing to pay. At this point, the highest bid price is only entered but not submitted to eBay. Do not hit the Place Bid button yet!

6. In the other browser window (the scope window), the Sniper sits and waits, scoping his item's bid activity. How does he scope his item? By repeatedly hitting the Refresh button in his browser. Each time the screen refreshes, any bids that may have been made by competing bidders would appear for that item. Remember, it is very important that both the browser screens are in view; the bid window and the scope window.

7. Twenty Seconds Away. With twenty seconds remaining in the auction for this item, the sniper really begins to sweat. This is it. All the planning will finally come to a head as the sniper makes his move. If the bid amount you tentatively entered in your bid window is still the highest bid for this item, countdown from ten and pound that Place Bid button. That's a snipe. Did you win?

Pssst. An alternative way of sniping an auction is by using the bid history page for an item. Instead of disabling graphics in your browser, and continuously refreshing the item page, you would refresh the bid history page and save yourself a step. Refreshing the bid history page is a lot more fun anyway.

Best Defense

How do you defend against the snipe? Well, now that you know this bid technique exists, and you're well versed on how it's actually done, it's time for you to jump into the fray. Here are some lines of defense against this controversial tactic.

Snipe Yourself

That's right. What's stopping you now from becoming a sniper? The best way to beat a sniper is to snipe them right back. Recent reports show that snipers typically win 60% of their auctions. Translation – close to half the time, snipers lose. With odds like that, you may have a fighting chance.

Max Out Your Proxy Bid

Take advantage of eBay's proxy bidding feature and really submit the highest you are willing to pay for this item should you win. By entering your highest amount, a sniper may still beat you - but who cares! You shouldn't be spending any more than you intended anyway – right?

Buy some Snipe Software

Nervous about sniping? Is sniping just not your bag? Why not get yourself some software that will do it for you? Here is a list of some of the options available to the snipe happy population online:

Auction Navigator

The AuctionNavigator is a Bidding, Sniping and Tracking program for buyers and sellers on eBay. AuctionNavigator places a bid in the closing seconds and sees to it that nobody outbids it.

Here's how! The software bids faster and more precisely than if you did it manually. Faster because AuctionNavigator exchanges compressed data with the eBay server, does not receive any graphics from eBay, automatically enters your eBay name and password and places bids during the very last seconds of the auction.

Visit AuctionNavigator's website at **http://www.auctionnavigator.com/index.html** and download the free trial version. There is also a free online tutorial available at the same website location.

Bidnapper

Why Bidnapper? Experienced eBay bidders use Bidnapper, the auction sniper software. With Bidnapper, you don't have to be at your computer at all hours of the day and night when the auction ends. Bidnapper keeps watch over your auction bidding 24/7, whether your computer is on or off. When it is time to bid, Bidnapper submits your bid at precisely the right moment, so there is no time for your bid to be countered. People who snipe eBay love this eBay auction sniping software! Visit their site at **http://www.bidnapper.com.**

SnipeRight

SnipeRight is an auction bidding and management program that places bids on auctions seconds before the auction ends such that your competitors don't have a chance to bid against you. This saves you money by not pushing up the price of the item. SnipeRight will only bid the absolute minimum required to win your auction, up to the Maximum bid you specify. SnipeRight was rated best sniper software by both PC Magazine and CPU Magazine. Visit them at **http://www.sniperight.com.**

iSnipeIt

iSnipeIt is an Auction Sniper! By automatically placing your bids at the last possible moments, iSnipeIt allows you to rest easy knowing that your competitors will have literally no time to react to your bid. Schedule your bid at your convenience and iSnipeIt places it with seconds to go, leaving you free to go about your business without worrying about when to bid next. Visit them at **http://www.isnipeit.com**.

AuctionStealer

A common complaint amongst those who fall victim to the snipe is that their Internet connection isn't fast enough. To mitigate these connection issues, online web based services like AuctionStealer are available. Think of it as someone bidding on your behalf on another computer. You can shut down your own computer go to sleep for the night and find out the next morning that AuctionStealer has successfully sniped an auction for you. Bottom line is that with web based options like AuctionStealer available, anyone can snipe an auction regardless of their Internet connection. Visit AuctionStealer at **http://auctioninsights.auctionstealer.com/home.cfm.**

ScamMaster I.Q. Review

Knowledge is power in the war on scammers. Here is your chance to test your scam I.Q. against the master himself; ScamMan.

Questions

1. What is Sniping?

2. True or False. Internet Explorer can be tweaked to improve Sniping performance.

3. Refreshing the _____ ______ page is another way of improving your odds at sniping.

4. True or False. Sniping is against the rules of eBay.

5. What is the easiest way to avoid being sniped?

Answers

1. Bidder will place a winning bid seconds before an auction ends. 2. True. 3. Bid History. 4. False. 5. Using Proxy Bidding.

eBay Scams Presents

THE ADVENTURES OF

SCAMMAN

CHAPTER 14

Defect Reject Scam

Defect Reject Scam

This is not one of the most popular scams out there but it's definitely out there. If you're a seller (and I know most of us are) then you should definitely pay attention during this lecture. Mark all your possessions before you sell them. Record serial numbers where possible. Pull out your invisible ink pen! This will all make sense by the end of the chapter.

Scam Synopsis

Scammer purchases defective or refurbished goods from dealers outside of eBay. They then bid and/or purchase that exact same item on eBay. Once they pay the seller and receive the item, they claim the item is defective and request a refund. Fearing negative feedback, the seller complies and the scammer sends the seller the defective item, keeping the working model.

1. ScamMan purchases a refurbished, slightly defective, sold as-is stereo from a local stereo shop. The cost of this item is greatly reduced due to its condition coming in at a whopping $25.00. Although externally, the stereo looks fantastic, ScamMan is told that the insides need a lot of TLC.

2. Using advanced search techniques, ScamMan scours eBay looking for the exact item he just purchased – for sale on eBay.

3. ScamMan locates the exact model of his stereo in new but used condition selling for $600.00.

SCAM FLOW

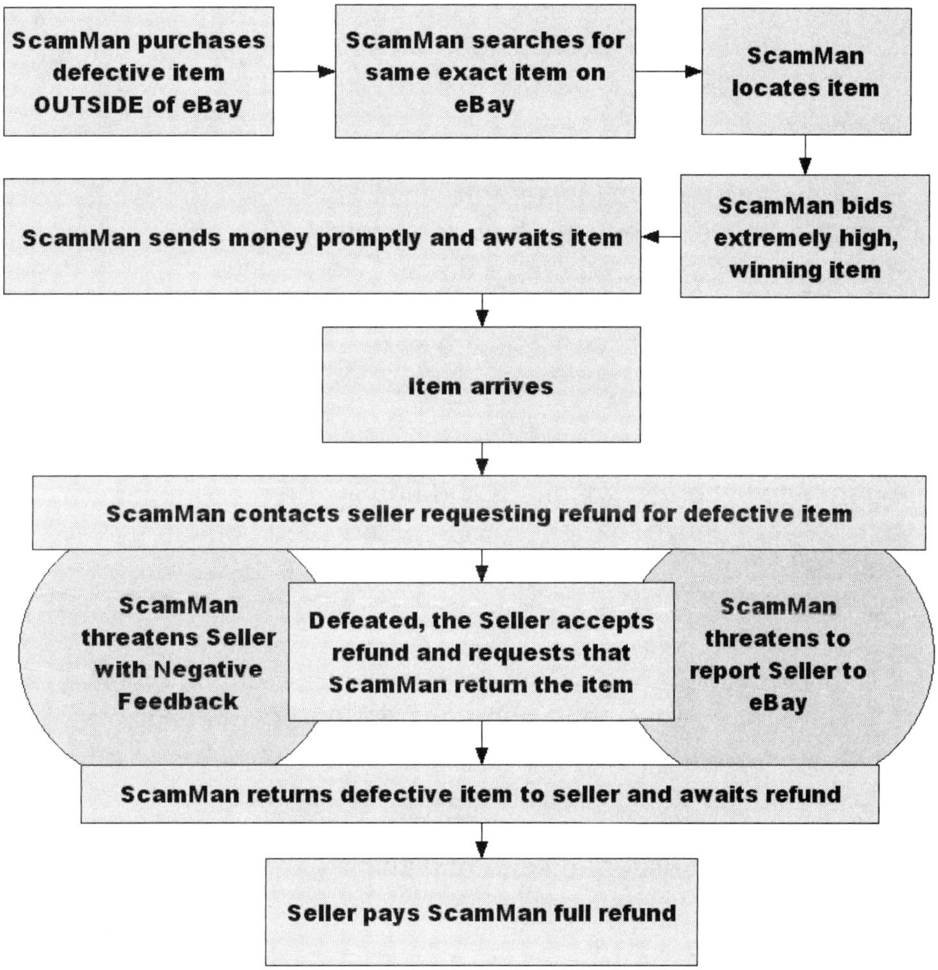
ScamMan purchases defective item OUTSIDE of eBay
ScamMan searches for same exact item on eBay
ScamMan locates item
ScamMan bids extremely high, winning item
ScamMan sends money promptly and awaits item
Item arrives
ScamMan contacts seller requesting refund for defective item
ScamMan threatens Seller with Negative Feedback
Defeated, the Seller accepts refund and requests that ScamMan return the item
ScamMan threatens to report Seller to eBay
ScamMan returns defective item to seller and awaits refund
Seller pays ScamMan full refund

4. ScamMan contacts the seller with various questions regarding the item to establish credibility.

5. Knowing that he'll be getting his money back, ScamMan bids high, ultimately winning the item.

6. ScamMan quickly pays the seller for the item and awaits the package at his home.

7. The Seller leaves positive feedback for ScamMan, praising him for being such a pleasure to deal with, and paying so promptly.

8. ScamMan receives the stereo and compares it to his defective model. They are a perfect match. The only difference being – ScamMan's doesn't work.

9. ScamMan politely contacts the seller by email letting him know that the item is defective and would like a refund.

10. When the confused seller questions ScamMan's story, ScamMan becomes impatient and angrily threatens to leave the Seller negative feedback. ScamMan even goes further to say he will report this seller to eBay and have his account suspended.

11. Fearing the tarnish of his otherwise stellar rating on eBay, the Seller acquiesces and agrees to refund ScamMan's money – once he receives the defective stereo.

12. ScamMan repackages the defective stereo in the same packaging the Seller had used and ships it back to its original address.

13. The seller receives the defective stereo and refunds ScamMan the entire amount of his winning bid price.

Best Defense

The best defence is a good offence so follow the next steps to protect yourself.

Mark It

To protect yourself from this type of scam, take the time to mark any item you sell with some sort of identifier - only you can see. Some people have suggested using invisible ink, while others have scratched the item in an unobvious location. Regardless of how you do it, mark it before it goes out the door so that if it comes back, you'll know its yours.

Serial Numbers

Depending on the type of item you are selling, it may or may not have a unique serial number attached to it. Take note of those numbers and store them. If the item is returned for defect related reasons, cross check the serial number to ensure it's the same item you shipped.

Visible Markings

Does your item have any distinct visible markings? Any scratches, scuffs or stains? Maybe the item is missing a tag, knob or screw. Make note of these visible markings and keep them on file - just in case!

Snap It

Last but not least, always make it a habit to actually take your own pictures rather than using stock photography or manufacturer provided images. When creating your listing, shoot photographs of your item from all angles and make sure to include any shots of marked or unique areas. For example, if the iPod you are selling has a small scratch on the back, photograph and display it in your listing for the world to see. This will deter scammers from attempting to swap it out by pulling the dreaded Defect Reject scam.

ScamMaster I.Q. Review

Knowledge is power in the war on scammers. Here is your chance to test your scam I.Q. against the master himself; ScamMan.

Questions

1. Why is it important to mark your items?

2. Noting an item's unique _______ _______ will help protect against the Defect Reject scam.

3. Why shouldn't you use stock photography for you items?

4. True or False. Defect Reject is one of the most popular scams on eBay.

5. What is the seller's motivation for giving the buyer a refund?

Answers

1. If it comes back, you'll know it's yours. 2. Serial number. 3. By using actual photos you can note the ways that it is distinct. 4. False. 5. Avoid negative feedback.

eBay Scams Presents

THE ADVENTURES OF

SCAMMAN

CHAPTER 15

Spamming

Spamming

As you probably already know, spamming is the practice of sending unsolicited e-mail messages, usually in a bulk format. Typically, spam in its most common state is delivered as a form of commercial advertising. All of us have most likely been on the receiving end of some spam. Our inboxes are polluted with these messages and it seems there's no end in sight. Well – things just got worse. Scammers are now using eBay to get to our email addresses. What they do with them is a whole other story.

Scam Synopsis

Scammers will fraudulently use the "Ask Seller a Question" link to obtain that member's email address. Once the email address is in their possession, they either use it to hijack that member's account, or sell the email address for a profit.

1. Unsuspecting seller creates listing for an item.

2. ScamMan, on his routine surf-by on eBay, spots this item and clicks on the "Ask the Seller a Question" link.

3. On the Ask the Seller a Question page, ScamMan types a very basic query. He then submits the question.

4. The innocent seller receives the query by email. The question being asked is actually already answered in the seller's listing. Paying that no mind, the Seller responds to the query.

SCAM FLOW

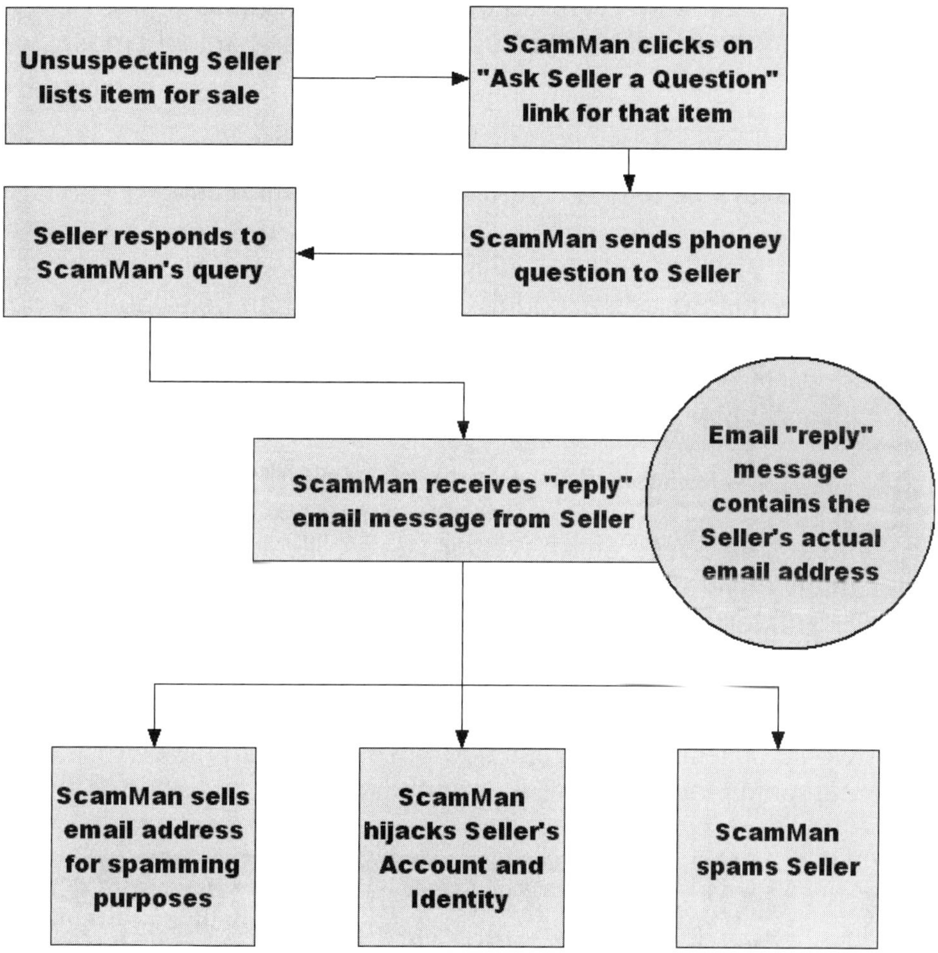
Unsuspecting Seller lists item for sale
ScamMan clicks on "Ask Seller a Question" link for that item
ScamMan sends phoney question to Seller
Seller responds to ScamMan's query
ScamMan receives "reply" email message from Seller
Email "reply" message contains the Seller's actual email address
ScamMan sells email address for spamming purposes
ScamMan hijacks Seller's Account and Identity
ScamMan spams Seller

Pssst. You may also notice that no where does it actually show the Seller's email address. Using the Ask the Seller a Question page does not initially reveal a member's email address.

5. When ScamMan receives the reply email message from the Seller, the email header reveals the Seller's actual email address.

6. With this information in hand, ScamMan has several options available to him. Here are a some of the most popular:

- Hijack this Seller's account. Easier said than done but having this members User ID and actual email address is a great start. Hijacking accounts will be discussed in more detail in a later chapter.
- Sell the Email Address. Assuming ScamMan has pulled this scam on more than one member, he more than likely has quite a database of email addresses collected. There are many buyers (spammers) for this type of information and ScamMan can make a handsome profit selling them off.
- Spam Members. Similar to the previous example, ScamMan most likely has done this to a number of people already. He would collect all the email addresses and start his own spam campaign terrorizing eBay members across the world.

Pssst. Here's an example of an email a scammer would send attempting to sell his eBay list of email addresses.

> *To whom it may concern,*
>
> *We are selling an email database filled with eBay member contact information. These represent both sellers, buyers and shoppers and please also note – over 90% of eBay customers are also PayPal users!*
>
> *This database contains over 553 User IDs and email addresses collected over the last 3 months. We keep this database updated constantly and ensure these are valid on a quarterly basis.*
>
> *We will deliver this database to you in any format you prefer, i.e. Excel, Text, Word, ASCII, etc.).*
>
> *The price for this database is $450.00 (USD). You can pay by PayPal, check or money order.*
>
> *Please contact me by emailing IamAscammer@scamming.com*
>
> *Thank you for reading,*
>
> *ScamMan and my scamming friends*

Best Defense

Defending yourself against spammers can be a difficult task. They're a sneaky bunch and it seems that every time we come up with some line of defense, they break through it. Regardless, the suggestions listed below will definitely be of some assistance in our ongoing fight against the spam.

Separate Email Account

To really avoid this scam from happening to you, simply create a separate email address for all your eBay activity. That's it. It's as easy as that. Most ISPs (Internet Service Providers) provide subscribers with multiple email address options. Now, when you respond to a member's query, they will only see the email address you use for eBay and not the one you use normally. Always stipulate in your response that this email account is only for outgoing mail. You will not respond to emails that are sent directly to it. If this member has any other questions, they are to return to the Ask the Seller a Question link on the actual item page.

Things to Watch Out for…

To best protect yourself, be especially leery of the following types of questions that may come your way:

- Really Stupid Questions. Sometimes it can be painfully obvious that the scammer is simply trying to get you to respond so that he can steal your email address. No example required. You'll know its stupid when you get one.
- Redundant Questions. Why would someone ask what color your item is when your listing not only shows a picture (in full color) but also states it in the description. Be smart. That's a "delete" situation if I ever did see one.
- Personal/Unrelated Questions. Scammers can be extremely slippery people. They may even attempt to appeal to your soft, human side. If you get personal questions sent your way, these too can be attempts on your email address. Steer clear and keep your delete key well oiled. Examples of personal questions that might come your way are as follows:

- Beautiful listing. Did you create it yourself?
- Hey! – I'm from California too. Where are you from exactly?
- Have you had a lot luck selling those tough market eh?
- Great movie – did you see the sequel?
- I love that designer too. Did you see his latest stuff?

Too Late – Now What?

If you bought this book too late and you're already a victim of spam, here are some things you can do to combat the problem:

Adjust Your Notification Preferences

On you're my eBay page, you can completely control the types of emails that come your way – at least those coming from eBay. To access this notification page, simply click on the My eBay link in the eBay main toolbar. On the My eBay page, scroll down to the My Account section on the left-hand side of the screen. There, you will see a link for eBay Preferences. Go ahead and click on that link. At the top of the list, you will see an option for Notifications. Click on the view/change link. Based on your own preferences, enable or disable options from the list of notifications available.

Report It

If you've been spammed – eBay wants to know. Not only do they want to know, they want to know ALL the juicy details. To contact eBay, simply click on the Help button on the eBay main toolbar. On the left-hand side of the screen, go ahead and click on the Contact Us link. eBay can't stop them if they don't hear about it. Do us all a favor and let them know.

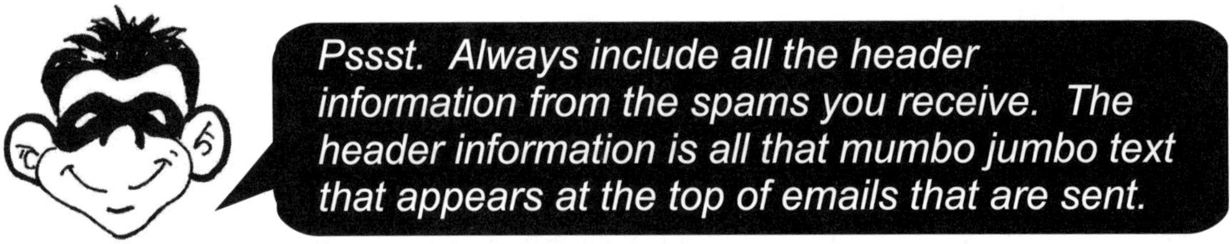

Filter It

Most email programs today (i.e. Microsoft Outlook, Netscape Messenger, etc.) include a feature which blocks spam from your inbox. By setting up filters or rules, spam will be deleted or rerouted before you even see it. For more information on your email program's filtering abilities, please contact the manufacturer's help documentation or support line.

Spam Bashing Software

When all else fails, sometimes you just have to spend some money to resolve a problem. A whole slew of software utilities exists that combat this very problem. Visit PCWorld.com to download spam busting trial versions of these utility programs.

SpamCatcher

Use SpamCatcher to destroy spam by developing rules that target and blacklist bulk email.

SpamKiller v4.0

SpamKiller version 4.0 will stop spam dead in its tracks and, as an added bonus, let the sender know about it too!

Spam Alarm v2.0

Stop unwanted messages by filtering them against 15,000 spam messages.

SpamNet for Outlook v3.0

Easy to use, no frill tool that helps reduce spam in Microsoft Outlook.

HateSpam v3.2.153

This is a filter add-on for Microsoft Outlook that eliminates junk mail with its many robust features.

Ignore It

Never reply to spam – never. Don't even "unsubscribe" when prompted. You may have noticed that most spam emails have a message at the very bottom that states something like the following:

To stop receiving emails from Spammers Inc. or to change your Spammers Inc. subscriptions, go here. You are registered as: Spam@hater.com

Don't do it! Anytime you actually reply to a spam message, you are confirming with that spammer that your email address is indeed valid. Once they get that response, they simply move you to their database to later sell at a premium. No replies. Just deletes.

Avoid Contests

Do your best to resist the urge to enter contests or lotteries where an email address is requested. These sometimes free giveaways are anything but. Instead, they take your contact information (including your email address) and sell it to the highest bidder. Keep your email address close to your chest and guard it with your life.

ScamMaster I.Q. Review

Knowledge is power in the war on scammers. Here is your chance to test your scam I.Q. against the master himself; ScamMan.

Questions

1. What is spamming?

2. True or False. The Ask the Seller a Question page reveals a member's email address.

3. What's the easiest way to defend yourself from spammers?

4. What are two of the four types of questions to watch out for when you receive queries via e-mail?

5. Where on eBay's site can you report spammers?

Answers

1. The practice of sending unsolicited e-mail messages, usually in a bulk format. 2. False. 3. Use a separate e-mail account for eBay transactions. 4. Stupid, redundant, unrelated or personal questions. 5. The Contact Us section of Help.

eBay Scams Presents

THE ADVENTURES OF

SCAMMAN

CHAPTER 16

Second Chance Scam

Second Chance Scam

Everybody loves a second chance in life. It's no different on eBay. The problem here is that a second chance on eBay can sometimes be a scam in disguise. This one is so simple in its execution, that it makes you wonder how you would ever fall for it. Believe me when I say though – many do, my friends, many do.

Scam Synopsis

Shortly after losing an auction, the second place bidder is contacted by the "seller" claiming that the winning bidder disappeared, leaving the item available. The happy bidder transfers money to the email address provided which is later discovered to NOT be that of the real seller.

1. ScamMan scans recently completed auctions on eBay looking for big ticket items. He is also looking for items where there were more than one bidder involved.

2. Upon finding said auction, ScamMan checks that item's bid history. He is looking for second or third place bidders who actually lost out on this auction item.

3. Spotting the second place loser for this item, ScamMan clicks on the members User ID (in the Bid History list) and then proceeds to click on the Contact Member link.

4. In his email to the losing bidder, ScamMan types the following text:

SCAM FLOW

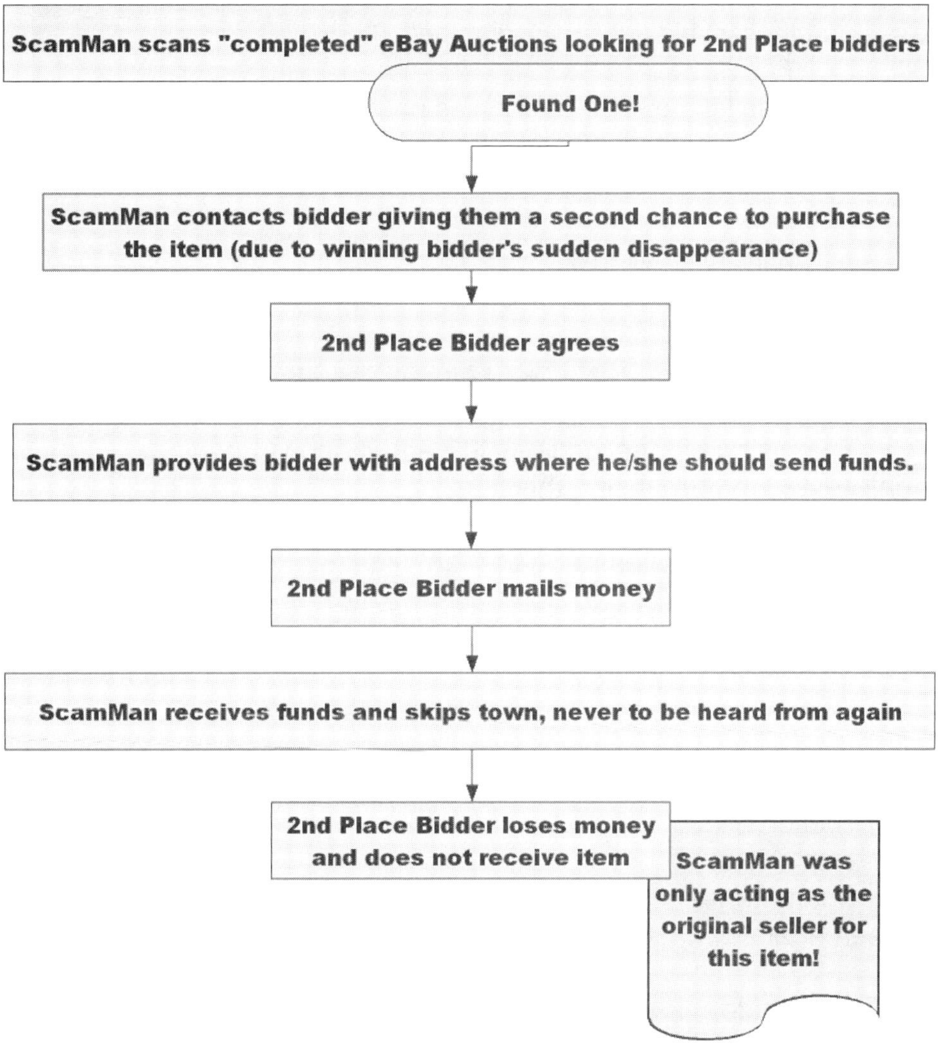
ScamMan scans "completed" eBay Auctions looking for 2nd Place bidders
Found One!
ScamMan contacts bidder giving them a second chance to purchase the item (due to winning bidder's sudden disappearance)
2nd Place Bidder agrees
ScamMan provides bidder with address where he/she should send funds.
2nd Place Bidder mails money
ScamMan receives funds and skips town, never to be heard from again
2nd Place Bidder loses money and does not receive item
ScamMan was only acting as the original seller for this item!

> Dear "User ID",
>
> Are you still interested in purchasing this item? The winning bidder for this auction completely disappeared and will not respond to any of my emails. I've since contacted eBay to report him. My item is now back up for grabs and I noticed that you were next in line with the highest bid. I would be happy to sell you this item at the last bid price you submitted.
>
> Please let me know as soon as possible because there are several other bidders for this item that may be interested.
>
> Thanks for your time,
>
> ScamMan

5. The losing bidder receives the email and is definitely interested in purchasing this item.

6. The bidder replies to ScamMan's message letting him know that he is wiling to purchase the item at his last bid price amount.

7. ScamMan responds with payment instructions.

8. The bidder sends/transfers the funds as per ScamMan's instructions.

9. ScamMan receives the funds and skips town, never to be seen again.

10. The bidder loses his money and does not receive the item.

11. eBay will not assist the bidder in this situation because this transaction was completed outside of eBay's walls.

Best Defense

The real rub here is that second chance offers do occur – legitimately on eBay. eBay offers a system wherein sellers can contact losing bidders for another crack at their item when the winning bidder does not pay. So – how can you defend yourself against this scam? How can you tell when it's "too legit to quit" or "scammer time" (homage to MC Hammer)? Let's take a look.

eBay's Second Chance Process & Policy

eBay's process and policy is quite clear when it comes to legitimate second chance offers. You can access eBay's policies on second chance offers by clicking Help at the top of eBay's main page. Once the help screen appears, type "second chance offer" in the search box and then click Search.

Bottom-line is that if the seller is using eBay's built-in feature for second chance offers then you will not have any problems. It will be obvious to you that this offer is coming through eBay's system and not a seller's personal email account. Even if the user uses the Contact Member link, this is not the process eBay encourages sellers to use. Ask the right questions to ensure this is a legitimate offer.

Contact eBay

If you're ever in doubt of a second chance offer that has come your way, contact eBay directly. They will let you know if the offer is truly legitimate or just a low down dirty scam.

The Name of the Game

Although obvious, I still think this is worth mentioning. When you receive an offer for a second chance on an item, cross-check the user's name in the email to that of the actual seller on the listing page. Do they match? They should. There are always cases where members legitimately have more than one User ID but it should definitely raise a flag.

Source It

If you're technically savvy, track the email to its source IP address. Make sure that the seller's country of origin on the listing page matches up with the source IP address of the email.

Wire Transfers

Many of the more fraudulent second chance offers will state that the only payment method the seller accepts is by money wire transfer. Very legitimate services like Western Union and MoneyGram are used as vehicles of deceit as money is transferred from an unsuspecting bidder to a scammer. Cash transferred this way is almost impossible to track and the bidder always comes out losing their shirt in the process.

All this to say – avoid any second chance offers that only accept money wire transfers as a payment method.

Spellling and Grammmar

Always be leery of any communications that come your way riddled with spelling and grammar errors. It's no secret that many scams are pulled by non-english speaking individuals from foreign countries around the world - and this is sometimes quite clear by their emails. This is not to say that people with poor English skills are all scammers but it's definitely a red-flag waver and should be investigated further.

Spoofers

Unfortunately, with all the tips I've listed in this chapter, the scammers keep getting trickier and smarter every day. Using familiar phishing techniques, scammers will recreate eBay's Second Chance offer web page and send them through to a bidder – disguised as eBay. Fooled by the spoofed web page, bidders will fall for these scammer's advances and send money through for the item. See the Phishing chapter for more information on how you can defend yourself against the spoof scenario.

Rookies R Us

Scammer prey on the weak. That may be you. Weak prey for a scammer, especially when pulling this scam, is how new you are to eBay.

New members are definitely targets because they haven't really got the swing of things yet and may not be as careful in their dealings. Scammers can tell if you're a rookie by checking the number of transactions/feedback points you have. The number is right there, for the whole world to see, next to your User ID in the bid history for that listing item. The lower your number, the less experience you have buying and selling on eBay.

If you are in fact a rookie – don't act like one. Read this book, take notes and most of all, practice what you read.

Pssst. eBay makes it even easier for scammers to find the rookies by placing an icon next to their User IDs. For the first 30 days after joining eBay or changing an eBay User ID, members currently receive a small icon next to their feedback score. It might as well be a bull's-eye. Oh well.

Multiple Emails

In some cases, you may even get more than one second chance offer email for an item you've bid on and lost. In these cases, these people are not necessarily claiming to be the actual seller of that specific item but a similar seller with the same item for sale. Regardless of how great the price is – stay away from any offers that do not come through eBay's safe and protected pages. You're completely on your own when those deals fall sour.

Pix It

I love this one. I can't tell you how many times I've used this technique to ward off scammers and it always works. To truly verify if a seller actually has the item they are offering you a second chance on, ask them for a photograph. Ask them to send you a real close up picture of a certain part of the item, like the serial number plate or the on/off switch. If they are unable to do so for whatever lame reason, it's time to walk away from this scammer before you get pinched.

Ask for close-up pix like this!

ScamMaster I.Q. Review

Knowledge is power in the war on scammers. Here is your chance to test your scam I.Q. against the master himself; ScamMan.

Questions

1. How does a scammer find out what an other member bid on a certain item?

2. How does a scammer get in touch with second place losers for an item auction?

3. True or False. There are legitimate second chance offers through eBay.

4. What are two things you can do to avoid this scam?

5. How can asking for photos ward off this type of scam?

Answers

1. Using bid history. 2. Using bid history, the scammer identifies who the other bidders were. To contact them, he uses the Contact Member link. 3. True. 4. Never deal outside of eBay, Contact eBay's Safe Harbor, Avoid Wire Transfers, Ensure the name on the email matches the seller's user ID. 5. To truly verify if a seller actually has the item they are offering you a second chance on, ask them for a photograph.

eBay Scams Presents

THE ADVENTURES OF

SCAMMAN

CHAPTER 17

Phantom Bidding

Phantom Bidding

Cool name. Shameful scam. This one is very similar to the Shilling scam with one big difference – there are no associates. Think of Phantom Bidding as the loner's version of Shilling. Unfortunately, this scam is really easy to do, requires very little setup and is very difficult to prosecute. Does that mean we should give up? Absolutely not. Who ya gonna call? PhantomBusters!

Scam Synopsis

A seller inflates the bid price of his own item by bidding against himself under a different User ID.

Pssst. Nothing stops eBay members from having several User IDs on eBay. eBay is doing their best though to crack down on those people doing it for the wrong reasons. Email addresses from sites like Hotmail and Yahoo! are no longer good enough – on their own. Here is an excerpt from their registration screen that really shows how tight their security is becoming:

Registration is free. However, a credit card is needed to confirm your identity and keep eBay safe. Your card will not be charged or shared with eBay sellers.

Don't want to put your card on file?

Enter a different email instead, as long as your new email is from an Internet Service Provider (Sympatico, Rogers, etc.), company, school, or organization.

Verify your address by postal mail. We will mail a confirmation code to you, and you can complete registration when it arrives.

SCAM FLOW

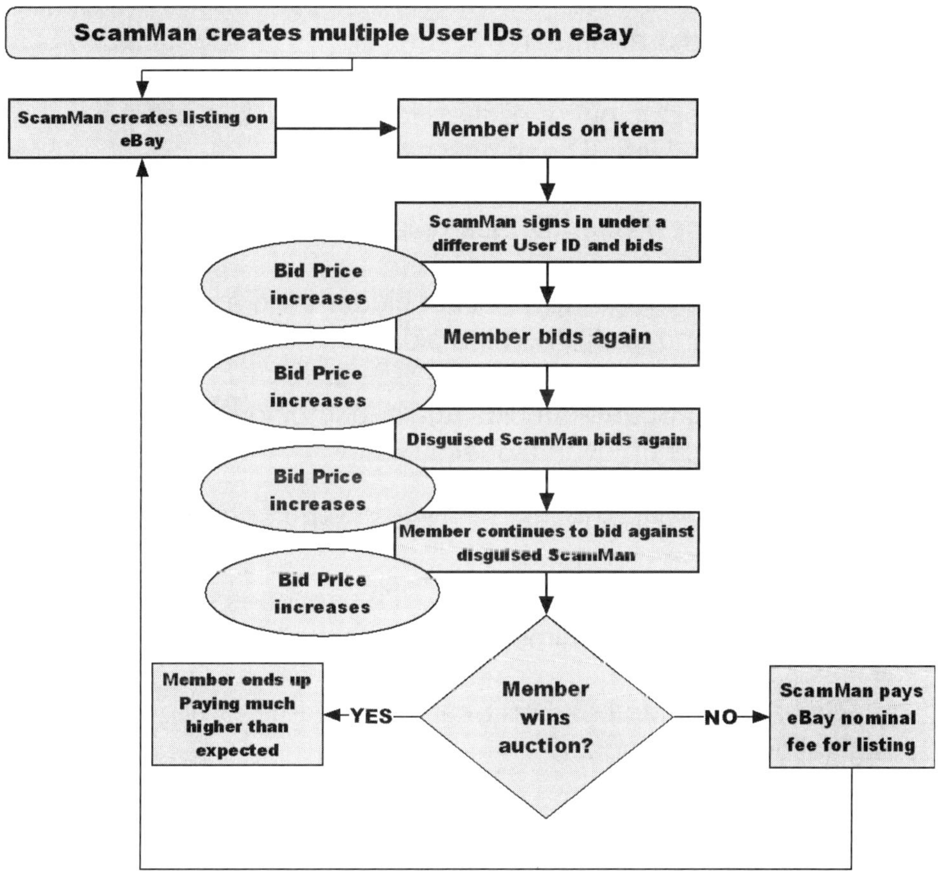
ScamMan creates multiple User IDs on eBay
ScamMan creates listing on eBay
Member bids on item
ScamMan signs in under a different User ID and bids
Bid Price increases
Member bids again
Bid Price increases
Disguised ScamMan bids again
Bid Price increases
Member continues to bid against disguised ScamMan
Bid Price increases
Member wins auction?
YES
Member ends up Paying much higher than expected
NO
ScamMan pays eBay nominal fee for listing

1. ScamMan registers himself again on eBay, under a different User ID. ScamMan now has two different identities on eBay.

2. As himself, ScamMan lists an item for sale on eBay.

3. Unassuming, innocent bidder bids on item.

4. No one else bids on this item. ScamMan grows impatient.

5. Auction end draws near.

6. ScamMan signs out of eBay. He signs back in using his alter ego sign-in User ID and password.

7. Under the new User ID, ScamMan bids on his own item.

8. Via proxy bidding, the innocent bidder's bid amount inches higher and is still the high bid.

9. A disguised ScamMan bids again, bumping the patsy bidder's bid price up even higher.

10. The unsuspecting bidder is still the high bidder though.

11. ScamMan (under his new User ID) continues to inch his bids up until ScamMan himself becomes the high bidder.

12. Sweat begins to bead on ScamMan's head. Will the original bidder, bid again?

13. Victory – the unsuspecting bidder bids again to beat the disguised ScamMan and ends up winning the auction.

Best Defense

Have you ever seen something so disgraceful? If you've been reading about the other scams out there, your answer is probably yes. This one isn't as tough as it seems to bust. Best Defense tips full steam ahead!

Know Your Limits

Know what you are willing to pay for an item and stick to it. Don't get caught up in auction hysteria. Check the web. How much is an item like this truly worth? Why pay more online, when you can walk into a store and buy it for less. Know your price and be a rock. Don't budge.

Bid Retractions

Keep an eye on auctions where bid retractions occur. This is typically a clear cut sign of a Phantom Bid in action. Try and imagine. Someone like ScamMan (under the guise of new User ID) bids too high and ends up the high bidder for an item he's phantom bidding on. Instead of following through, he simply retracts his bid, leaving the previous bidder as the high bidder again. Tricky, tricky, tricky.

Bid History

Check out the bid history for the item you are bidding on. Be wary of those bidders bidding against you with zero feedback points. Don't get me wrong, they may very well be legitimate – or not. In this case, ScamMan had just created that User ID, meaning it was probably showing zero in terms of feedback points. That was a dead giveaway in my opinion.

Private and Hidden

Keep your eyes open for those sellers who use hidden feedback or run private auctions. Those spell danger with a capital D. If the auction is private, that means bidder's identities are hidden, possibly hiding shillers and phantoms playing in the trenches.

Safe Harbor

Contact eBay at safeharbor@ebay.com. If you feel like you are falling victim to a Phantom bidder, let eBay know. There are several spots you can go to ring the bell. The key here is to let them know. They can't stop what isn't reported. Lastly, understand that eBay has more visibility into what is happening on the backend of any auction that is running. Let them tell you what's what.

Check Their Other Auctions

If you feel someone is Phantom bidding against you, check that bidder's other auctions. Take a look to see if that bidder is always bidding on a certain seller's auctions – namely the seller's auctions. Then, if you do see a trend, are they consistently raising bid amounts without actually winning?

Outside the Walls

Avoid the post auction close sale. Sometimes, what you'll see happen is a seller will contact you after their auction has closed. They will claim that the true winner didn't pay and that you were next on the list of bids. Will you still purchase the item at your last bid amount – which was artificially inflated anyway. Don't do it! Make it a rule to never deal outside of eBay. Do so at your own risk because eBay provides no protection for members who stray.

Feedback Phantom

Always check a bidder's feedback forum as well. What you're looking for here is a suspicious amount of positive feedback back and forth between the same seller and buyer. This can sometimes mean a seller and buyer are really the same person and there's an element of feedback padding happening. Be suspicious, be very suspicious.

ScamMaster I.Q. Review

Knowledge is power in the war on scammers. Here is your chance to test your scam I.Q. against the master himself; ScamMan.

Questions

1. What other scam is Phantom Bidding most like?

2. True or False. You can only have one User ID on eBay.

3. What safeguard has eBay put in place for people registering using Hotmail and Yahoo! email accounts?

4. Why do bid retractions and Phantom bidding sometimes go hand in hand?

5. What is hidden in a private auction?

Answers

1. Shilling. 2. False. 3. They must now register with a credit card as well. 4. When a phantom bidder goes too far, they sometimes win their own item. In those cases, they will attempt to retract their last bid in hopes of saving the auction. 5. Bidder's identities.

eBay Scams Presents

THE ADVENTURES OF

SCAMMAN

CHAPTER 18

Feedback Padding Scam

Feedback Padding Scam

Have you ever noticed those members on eBay that have feedback scores in the thousands? Well, many (and I do mean many) have worked very hard to attain that score and their business depends on it. Enter ScamMan. He does things a little differently. If there's a corner to cut, he'll cut it – without ever looking back. Looks like the scammers have found a way to make a good feedback rating meaningless.

Scam Synopsis

Scammers will buy and sell feedback in order to pad their feedback scores, creating a false sense of security for other members who deal with them.

1. ScamMan designs a listing on eBay for an e-book for sale. The listing is masterfully put together to look like a real item for sale. Truth be told though, the real item for sale is positive feedback for the scheming buyer.

Pssst. Most scammers who run this listing typically sell the same e-book, one entitled: MEGA FEEDBACK IN 7 DAYS. If you do a search on eBay for this e-book, you'll find plenty of scammers selling positive feedback to anyone willing to buy. Scammers don't discriminate.

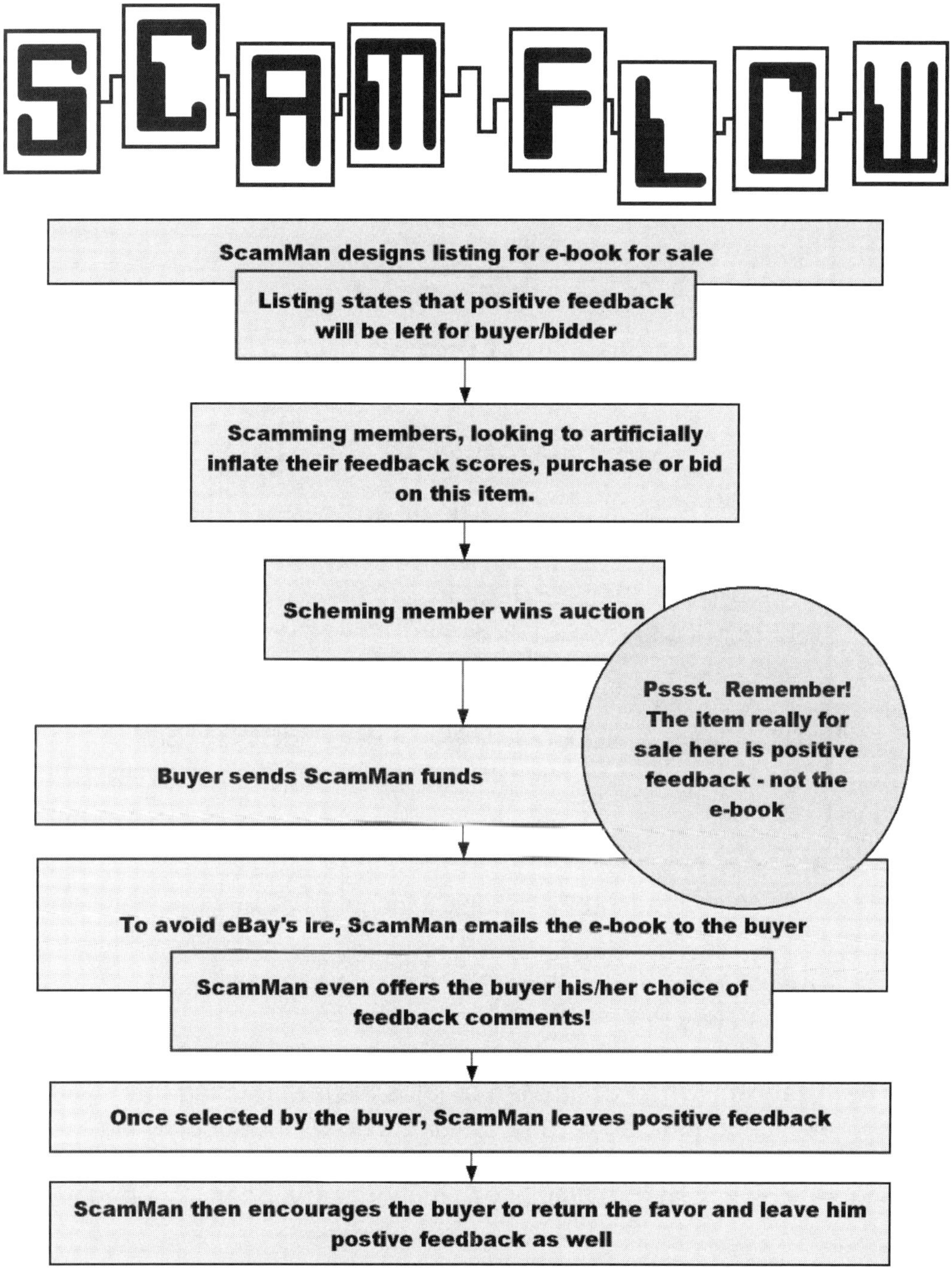
SCAM FLOW
ScamMan designs listing for e-book for sale
Listing states that positive feedback will be left for buyer/bidder
Scamming members, looking to artificially inflate their feedback scores, purchase or bid on this item.
Scheming member wins auction
Pssst. Remember! The item really for sale here is positive feedback - not the e-book
Buyer sends ScamMan funds
To avoid eBay's ire, ScamMan emails the e-book to the buyer
ScamMan even offers the buyer his/her choice of feedback comments!
Once selected by the buyer, ScamMan leaves positive feedback
ScamMan then encourages the buyer to return the favor and leave him postive feedback as well

Does it really bother you when no one bids on your items because your feedback score is too low? Everyone wants that big yellow star next to their name and you're no different. Don't let being new to eBay be a handicap. Instead, beat this unfair system by jacking up your feedback score - quickly and legally!

HERE'S HOW!

I am selling 50 copies of this e-book called:

MEGA FEEDBACK IN 7 DAYS!

The price per e-book is only 99 cents. For each e-book you purchase, I will leave you positive feedback. Its that simple. E-book for Feedback = Increase in eBay Sales!

Now that's an equation even math haters would love.

Bid with confidence!

A "Selling Feedback" Listing on eBay

2. There are two forms this eBay Feedback Padding scam can take. They are:

- **Auction**. When ScamMan creates his listing using the auction format, he is really setting it up so that people *bid* (rather than buy outright) his positive feedback. The same e-book is sold, but typically to the highest bidder. Depending on how much a positive feedback point is worth to you, this is how ScamMan makes his money.

- **Buy It Now.** Using this format of listing, ScamMan is actually selling his positive feedback to buyers – without the bidding process. In most cases, scammers using this format will sell large quantities from the one listing. Each time someone buys an “e-book”, positive feedback is left for that buyer and the quantity available decreases by one. Typically, scammers will sell feedback (e-books) at the buy it now price of 99 cents, with 50 available at any one time. They’ll even sweeten the offer by encouraging you to buy more than one by offering an additional e-book on another topic. What’s 99 cents right?

3. Choosing the auction route, ScamMan lists his item on eBay.

4. Scamming members began to bid on his e-book for sale.

5. Upon auction completion, the winning bidder send through his payment for the item.

6. To complete the transaction, ScamMan emails through the e-book to the winning bidder.

7. ScamMan, the courteous seller that he is, offers the winning bidder his choice of feedback comments. The options are as follows:

- One of eBay’s best! A real pleasure to deal with.
- Quick, polite and honest. A true asset to eBay.
- Great Communication, Quick Payment, Great Ebayer, A+++
- Wonderful transaction! Fast Payment! Thanks so much!!

8. The winning bidder selects his feedback from the shopping list of options.

9. ScamMan proceeds, as promised to leave this positive feedback for the seller.

10. ScamMan encourages the winning bidder to return the favor and leave positive feedback for him.

11. The winning bidder complies and everyone is happy – except the rest of the eBay population who keep getting scammed by these cretins.

Best Defense

We all know how important feedback is to the whole eBay process. When you bid on an item, you are always encouraged to check the seller's feedback score first – before you do anything. What this scam does is chip at and ultimately destroy the entire backbone to this online system. Without feedback you can count on, we have no way of really knowing who we're dealing with. Let's take a look at some ways you can help fight against this evil scrooge we like to call the Feedback Padding scam.

eBay Policy

It's against it. That's all I have to say. Ok, I lied. If you come across someone selling an item for next to nothing, and its obvious they are looking to buy and sell feedback, stay away. Stay far, far away. Help keep eBay's feedback system strong and credible by not joining this group of hooligans.

Check Feedback Forum

Scammers are counting on the fact that most bidders/buyers will not look at the seller's actual feedback forum but rather only the actual score of positives versus negatives. This is a very accurate assessment of how people do business on eBay. If the feedback score is high, this means the seller is credible and trustworthy. If the feedback score is low, the seller is new, inexperienced, potentially a scammer, stay away. If only it were this easy.

To really root out those scammers who are buying and selling feedback, check their feedback forums to really see where those points are coming from. For the item you are interested in buying, click on the seller's feedback score to enter their feedback forum. There, you will see all the feedback left for this seller as well as the actual item numbers for the auctions they've bought and sold. If most of the items are under a dollar, or you see lots and lots of cheap e-books, you've got yourself a scamming scammer waiting to scam you out of your hard earned dollars.

ScamMaster I.Q. Review

Knowledge is power in the war on scammers. Here is your chance to test your scam I.Q. against the master himself; ScamMan.

Questions

1. What "real" item is typically sent to a buyer purchasing feedback?

2. Explain "Auction" feedback padding.

3. Explain "Buy it now" feedback padding.

4. What is feedback padding also known as?

5. How can checking a seller's feedback forum help detect this scam?

Answers

1. E-book. 2. When a scammer creates his listing using the auction format, they are really setting it up so that people bid (rather than buy outright) the positive feedback. 3. Using this format of listing, a scammer is actually selling his positive feedback to buyers – without the bidding process. Typically, the feedback is sold at a set, fixed price. 4. Feedback Solicitation 5. If most of the items bought and sold are under a dollar, or you see lots and lots of cheap e-books changing hands.

eBay Scams Presents

THE ADVENTURES OF

SCAMMAN

CHAPTER 19

The Photo Doctor

The Photo Doctor

There's nothing worse than being misled by a picture. How many times have you seen an amazing picture of something for sale in a catalog, rushed to the store to make the purchase, only to find out that it looks completely different when you get there. Worse case scenario – you get back in your car, drive home and eat your dinner. On eBay, the outcome is not so rosy. Let's take a look.

Scam Synopsis

Scammers with expertise in computer photo editing, are doctoring photos of the items they are selling, misleading bidders into making a purchase.

1. ScamMan creates listing for an item for sale.

2. Using a digital camera, ScamMan takes pictures of his item for sale.

3. Once he's completed his photo shoot, ScamMan downloads all the images to his computer.

4. Using a photo editing software package, ScamMan doctors or modifies the images so that the item shows no imperfections, i.e. scratches, blemishes, or discolorations.

5. In his listing, ScamMan includes the following statements in a very small font, buried amongst a sea of text.

   Since falling victim to several refund related scams, I no longer offer refunds for my items. In light of this policy change, I stand behind my products 100% so please bid with confidence.

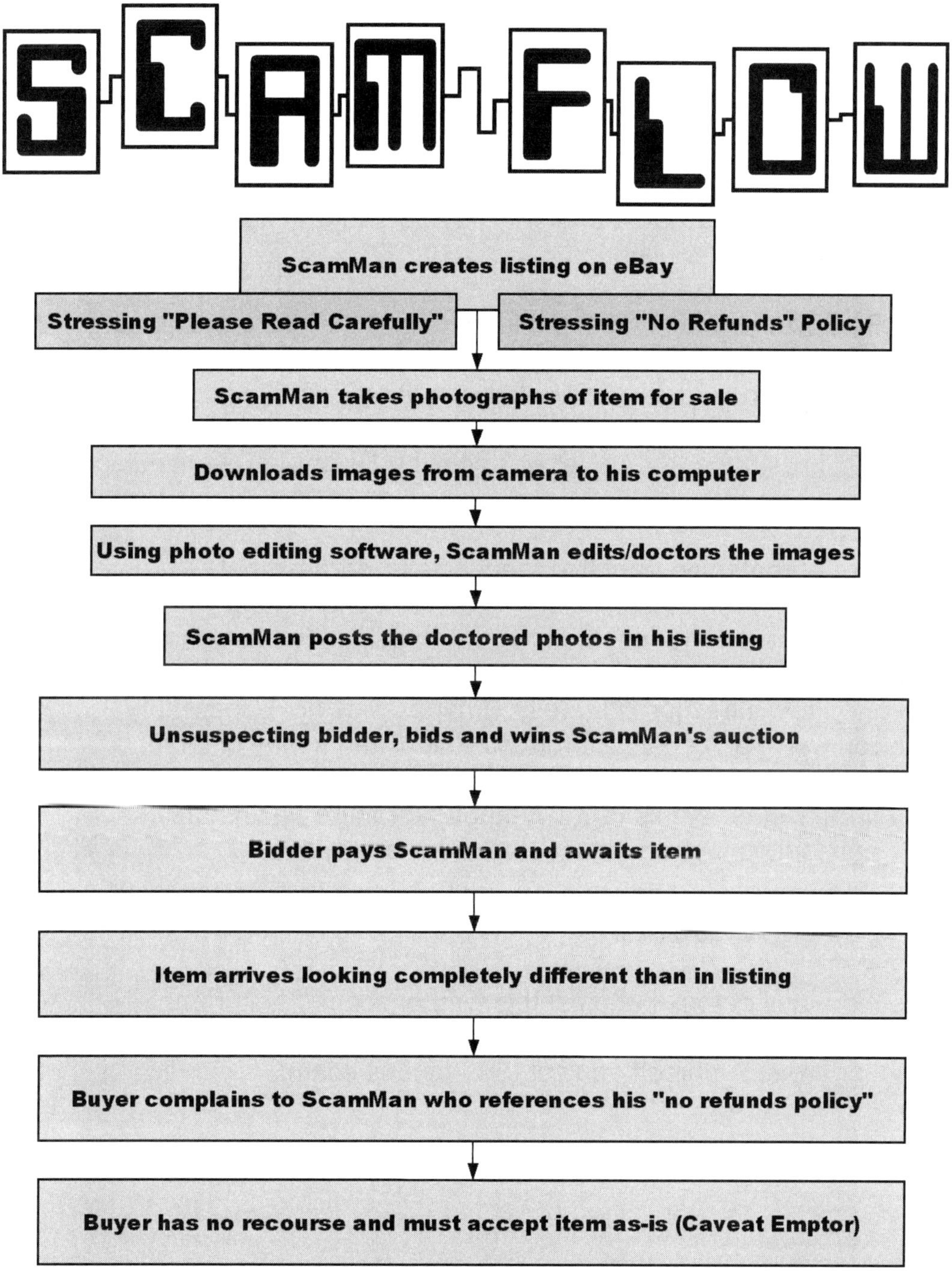
SCAM FLOW
ScamMan creates listing on eBay
Stressing "Please Read Carefully"
Stressing "No Refunds" Policy
ScamMan takes photographs of item for sale
Downloads images from camera to his computer
Using photo editing software, ScamMan edits/doctors the images
ScamMan posts the doctored photos in his listing
Unsuspecting bidder, bids and wins ScamMan's auction
Bidder pays ScamMan and awaits item
Item arrives looking completely different than in listing
Buyer complains to ScamMan who references his "no refunds policy"
Buyer has no recourse and must accept item as-is (Caveat Emptor)

6. ScamMan uploads his doctored images to his listing and the auction goes live.

7. Unsuspecting bidder bids on item, and ultimately wins the auction.

8. Buyer sends ScamMan his payment for the item and patiently awaits his prize.

9. Buyer receives item and immediately notices that it is not exactly what was depicted in the listing, i.e. photos in listing showed an item in much better condition.

10. Frustrated, the buyer contacts the ScamMan demanding a refund.

11. Threatening negative feedback for harassment, ScamMan reminds the buyer that his listing did not lie. All disclaimers were included to guard against this very issue. Next time, ScamMan muses, the buyer should read the listings a little more carefully. Images may not necessarily represent any specific product. Actual items may differ in specific properties and performance. Except as stated above, the designer of this listing cannot guarantee against any unintentional errors, inaccuracies, or omissions.

Best Defense

Is there any defense against this type of scam? Unfortunately – none that are foolproof. Here are a some things you can do to better protect yourself against this heinous scam.

Read Carefully

I've said it once, you know that I'll say it a thousand times – read the listings carefully. Remember, for the listing to be truly impenetrable, it must state somewhere disclaimers regarding omissions, bad photos, no refunds, etc. If it doesn't state these things, and you get scammed, at least you have a small, thin, almost feeble leg to stand on. That's better than no legs right?

If you see an item for sale that states – in small print – that pictures are not true representations of the item or no refund policy, then you must raise your red flag. Read the listings carefully and I don't care how long, or how small the font is – that's no excuse. Read it – and avoid the weep.

Ask Questions – Regardless

I say "regardless" because asking questions also gives you an idea of what kind of seller you are dealing with. If you have any doubts regarding a listing's photos or claims, email the seller and ask them some questions. If a seller is selling a rare first edition printing of a book you desire, email the seller to confirm it is indeed a first printing and that it's in mint condition – like the image shows in the listing. It doesn't hurt and at the very least you'll have something in writing in case things go south.

Know Thy Enemy

If you have no idea what these photo editors can actually do, how can you possibly defend yourself against these image doctoring maniacs? You can't! Here are just some of the things these scammers can do using this type of software – quickly and very easily!

- Remove unwanted people/objects from photographs:

BEFORE **AFTER**

Clean the table off!

- Remove brand names from items:

BEFORE **AFTER**

Goodbye Kenwood!

- Lift brand name from one item and place on another:

BEFORE **AFTER**

Hello Sony!

- Remove scratches/blemishes/imperfections from items:

BEFORE **AFTER**

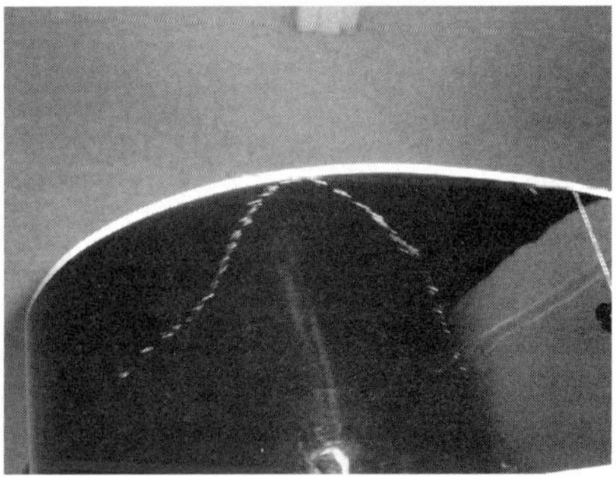

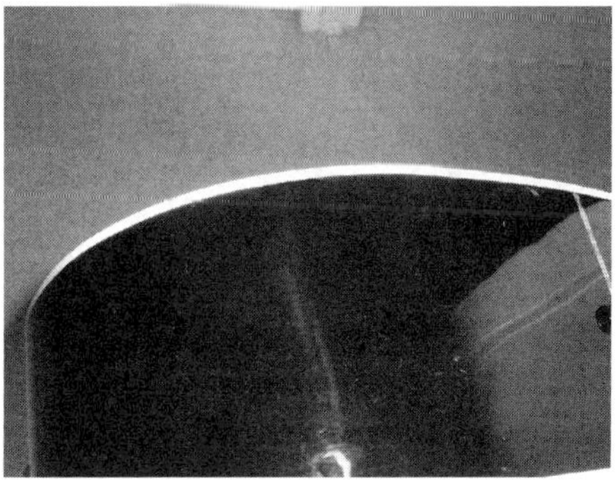

Guitar scratch vanishes!

- Change an item's color or pattern:

BEFORE

AFTER

Black t-shirt becomes a white one!

- Brighten items so they seem newer:

BEFORE

AFTER

From dark to light!

- Add lens flare to hide imperfections:

BEFORE **AFTER**

Flare obscures cracked car mirror

- Crop images so that only parts of an item are visible:

BEFORE **AFTER**

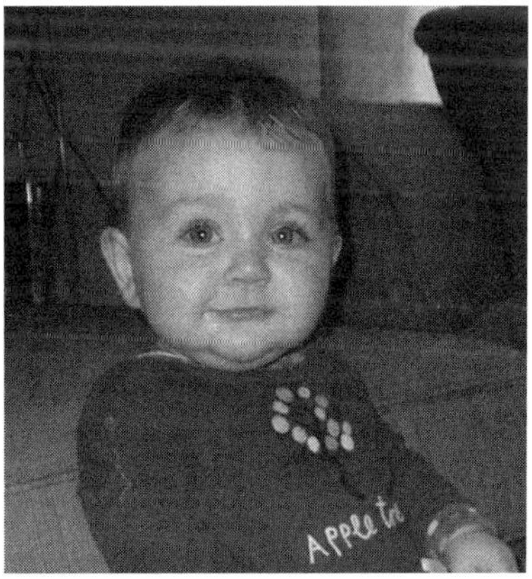

Goodbye Cereal Box!

- Place item on a different background, i.e. beach, Italy, etc.:

BEFORE

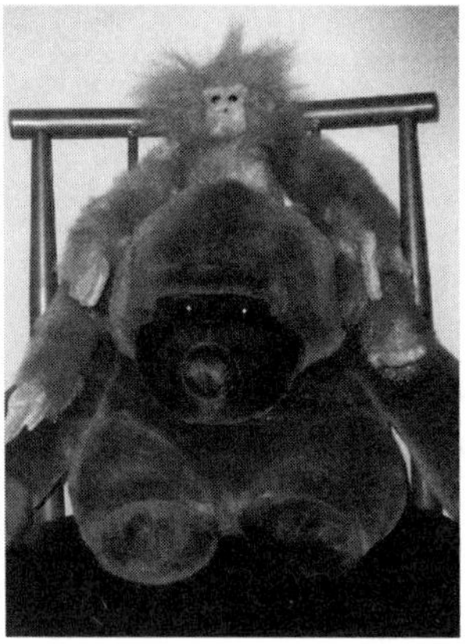

AFTER

Monkeys at the circus!

Know Thy Product

There are currently several software packages available that allow an individual to doctor and edit computer images. This software comes in all shapes and sizes and depending on your needs, there is most likely one customized for what you do. I recommend you visit these application's websites and download their free trial versions. By better understanding how these applications work, you will be one step ahead of the scammers who plan on using these weapons against you.

Corel PHOTO-PAINT

Visit Corel Corporation's website at www.corel.com and download the free trial version of CorelDRAW 12. Within this powerful suite of products is another application called Corel PHOTO-PAINT. This baby is one powerful monster of an application. With its incredibly robust set of features, it can do almost anything to your photographs.

Adobe Photoshop

You can truly explore the endless possibilities of photo editing using Adobe Photoshop. Visit them at www.adobe.com and download their free trial version of Adobe Photoshop Elements. You won't be disappointed.

JASC Paint Shop Pro

I love what's written on their website: The art of having fun - for those who want to have fun with their photos without learning advanced power tools. Visit JASC at www.jasc.com and click on their downloads link. There, you can download a free trial of Paint Shop Pro. Give it a try – you'll love it!

ScamMaster I.Q. Review

Knowledge is power in the war on scammers. Here is your chance to test your scam I.Q. against the master himself; ScamMan.

Questions

1. What kind of software can a scammer use to doctor/modify pictures?

2. Name three different ways a photo can be doctored in order to scam a buyer?

3. Why is it important to always read item descriptions carefully?

4. Name two different pieces of software that allow for this type of image doctoring.

5. What defense does a scammer typically use when confronted by his victim?

Answers

1. Photo Editor. 2. Remove unwanted people/objects from photographs, remove brand names from items, lift brand name from one item and place on another, remove scratches/blemishes/imperfections from items, change an item's color or pattern, brighten items, hide imperfections, crop mages, place on different backgrounds. 3. Scamming sellers will sometimes hide important disclaimers using small font sizes, faint colors or buried within a sea of text. 4. Corel PHOTO-PAINT, Adobe Photoshop, JASC Paint Shop Pro. 5. The listing did not lie.

eBay Scams Presents

THE ADVENTURES OF

SCAMMAN

CHAPTER 20

Win a Car Scam

Win a Car Scam

Are you one of those people who never wins anything? How tempting would it be if I told you the odds in winning are one in four? How about if the prize was a new car? I bet you're excited now! Well, cool your jets. This is yet another spoofer on the phish move, looking to scam your dollars. Translation – watch out. Things are never quite as they seem.

Scam Synopsis

eBay members are sent an email telling them that they can win a car. The email pretends to be sent from eBay, requesting your User ID and password in order to be entered into the draw. Once your information is captured, the scammer will use it to hijack your account or sell it to other heartless scammers. Needless to say – you're not going to win anything, let alone a car.

1. ScamMan creates graphical email that contains information on winning a new car. This email is extremely professional in its design and absolutely looks like its come from eBay. The email will sometimes outline the odds of winning (e.g. 1 in 4), what kind of prizes can be won (e.g. cars, money, etc.) and how easy it is to enter. By clicking on the link(s) at the bottom of the email, you are seconds from potentially winning.

2. ScamMan creates a "look-alike" eBay website. The link in the email will take them to this "spoof" site where they will be asked to enter their eBay User ID and password.

3a. ScamMan purchases a database of stolen eBay member email addresses.

SCAM FLOW

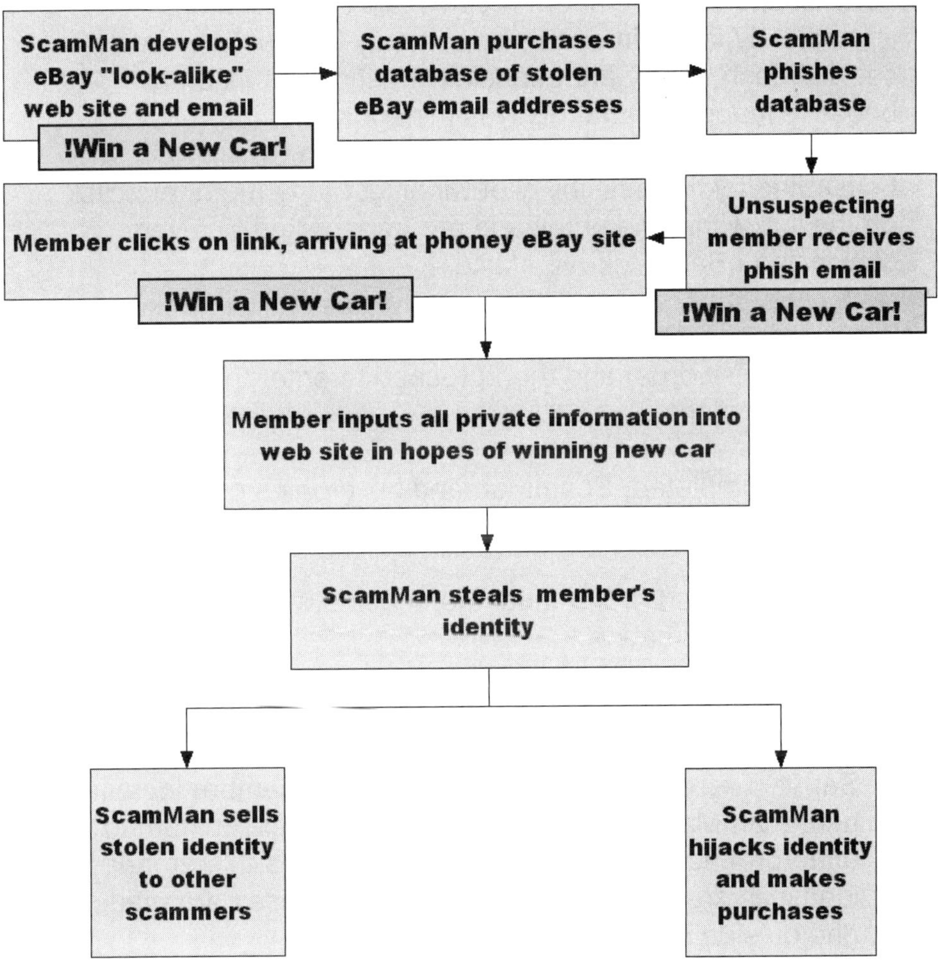
ScamMan develops eBay "look-alike" web site and email
!Win a New Car!
ScamMan purchases database of stolen eBay email addresses
ScamMan phishes database
Unsuspecting member receives phish email
!Win a New Car!
Member clicks on link, arriving at phoney eBay site
!Win a New Car!
Member inputs all private information into web site in hopes of winning new car
ScamMan steals member's identity
ScamMan sells stolen identity to other scammers
ScamMan hijacks identity and makes purchases

3b. ScamMan steals member's email addresses himself using the "Ask the seller a question" or "Contact a Member" feature on eBay.

4. With these addresses in hand, ScamMan emails the database using the fraudulent graphical email masquerading as an eBay representative.

5. Unsuspecting members receive this email and are immediately taken in by this opportunity to possibly win a free car and cash. They are especially trusting of this email because it appears that eBay is the sponsor.

6. Excited by the possibility of winning, many members click on the link within the email and are transported to a very convincing eBay "look-alike" site.

7. On this site, they are asked to sign-in (revealing their User IDs and passwords) and then proceed to enter their credit card information.

8. Once completed, ScamMan and his cronies collect this valuable and private information.

9. ScamMan and group must then decide what they want to do with the information.

They have two choices:

- Sell it. There is a huge market for eBay member identities and ScamMan can make a lot of money selling them to underground buyers. Once successfully sold, member's identities are in effect hijacked and purchases are made in and outside of eBay.

- Use it. Once an unsuspecting member submits their private information, ScamMan can hijack that user's account on eBay, and go on a buying spree. Keep in mind what we are talking about – credit card information, name, passwords and User IDs. You really wouldn't need anything else.

10. As the days pass, hijacked member begins to notice strange transactions appearing on their credit card bills. They may also notice that their sign-in name and password no longer work on eBay.

11. They immediately contact eBay only to find out that the email and website were fraudulent – not coming from eBay's servers.

12. The victimized eBay member is now forced to go through the tedious process of retrieving their lost account and funds.

Best Defense

The defense against this type of phishing and spoof site scenario is much the same as those described in detail in the Phishing chapter. Instead of re-listing all the details from that chapter, I will present you with a checklist of defense strategies and tips. If you require more information on any of the points listed, please refer to the chapter called Phishing.

☑ *Do not respond*

Never respond to email requests for personal information. Never.

☑ *Do not click*

Don't click on web links within emails. Instead, always type the actual website URL into your address bar.

☑ *Check the Greeting*

If an email or website is requesting personal information, it will almost never greet you in a general way. Avoid those emails that begin with Welcome Member. You have a name. They should be using it.

☑ *Encryption*

Look for the yellow lock that appears in the status bar of your browser. Any site where you're entering personal information should have an encryption lock displayed.

☑ *Stay on top of your finances*

Noticing strange activity on your credit/debit card statements? Could be a scammer. Review them often.

☑ *Get the Toolbar*

Avoid spoofed sites using eBay's Account Guard feature. It's built right into their free downloadable toolbar.

☑ *Be leery of attachments*

Avoid the Trojans that come hidden in email attachments. They could be reporting your every move to a scammer.

☑ *Virus Checkers*

Keep your checker up to date. Many virus checkers come with firewalls diminishing your chances of becoming a mark for one of these scammers.

ScamMaster I.Q. Review

Knowledge is power in the war on scammers. Here is your chance to test your scam I.Q. against the master himself; ScamMan.

Questions

1. What is a "spoof" email?

2. What are two different ways a scammer could get eBay members' email addresses?

3. What should you always do – instead of clicking on a link in an email that is sent you?

4. How can you tell if the site you are visiting is encrypted?

5. What is the name of eBay's spoof detector, built into their downloadable toolbar?

Answers

1. A "spoof" email is a fraudulent or fake email that appears to be from someone other than the actual sender. 2. Use Ask Seller a Question link, and await reply OR buy database of member email addresses on the black market. 3. Actually re-type the URL in your browser or enter the actual site through the homepage link. 4. A small "locked" lock appears in your browser's status bar at the bottom of your screen. 5. Account Guard

eBay Scams Presents

THE ADVENTURES OF

SCAMMAN

CHAPTER 21

The Shield Scam

The Shield Scam

Sounds like a comic book doesn't it? Well, there's nothing funny about this scam. This is yet another swindle where two "associates" come together to dupe you out of your hard earned cash. There are some pretty obvious red flags that come up letting you know it's happening – but it's usually too late at that point. Let's take a look.

Scam Synopsis

This scam involves one scammer entering a low bid on an eBay auction, and then a second scammer entering a bid that is high enough to scare other bidders away. Then, at the last minute, the second scammer retracts their bid and the first scammer wins – at their initial low price bid.

1. ScamMan menacingly roams the caverns of eBay searching for his next prey.

2. He finds the item he wants -a new TV, valued at $800. The opening bid on this item is a meager $99.00.

3. ScamMan bids $1000. The auction lists a bid of $99.99 as the highest bid as nobody else had yet bid on the item.

4. ScamMan quickly contacts his dirty, scum sucking counterpart – Scummy. He asks his pal Scummy to bid on this same item.

5. With a snicker, Scummy bids on this item at $990. The bid price jumps to $1000 (via proxy bidding) and ScamMan is still on top with this outrageously high bid price.

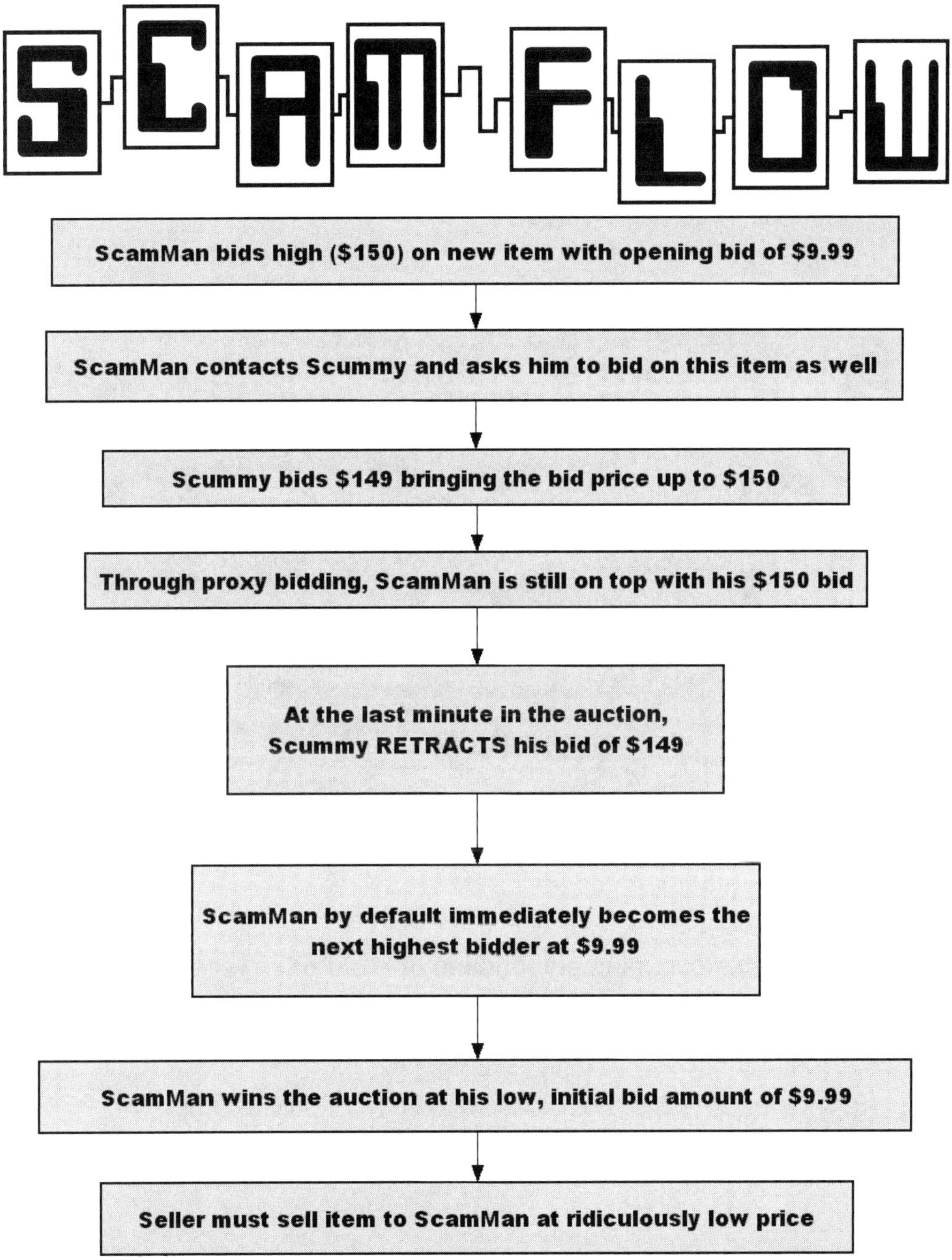
SCAM FLOW
ScamMan bids high ($150) on new item with opening bid of $9.99
ScamMan contacts Scummy and asks him to bid on this item as well
Scummy bids $149 bringing the bid price up to $150
Through proxy bidding, ScamMan is still on top with his $150 bid
At the last minute in the auction, Scummy RETRACTS his bid of $149
ScamMan by default immediately becomes the next highest bidder at $9.99
ScamMan wins the auction at his low, initial bid amount of $9.99
Seller must sell item to ScamMan at ridiculously low price

6. Other bidders who come across this listing are quickly deterred by the extra high bid price.

7. No one else bids on this item.

8. At the last minute, before the auction ends, Scummy retracts his high bid of $990.

Pssst. If you're wondering what a bid retraction is, here's a very quick and dirty explanation. eBay allows, under very exceptional circumstances, bidders to retract a bid they submitted on a listing on eBay. These exceptional circumstances are as follows:

- *Typos. You entered $999.99 instead of $9.99. Ouch.*
- *Description Changes. The description of the item changes significantly during the course of the auction.*
- *MIA. The seller cannot be reached.*
- *Hijack. Someone has hijacked your account and is bidding as you.*

9. When this occurs in any auction, the bid price reverts to the previous bidder's initial bid amount. In this case, that was $99.00.

10. ScamMan wins the TV at the paltry price of $99.00

Best Defense

As I stated in the introduction to this scam - it isn't that difficult to spot. The challenge is spotting it – in time. There is some good news to share. With eBay's new retraction rules, this scam is nearly dead.

Check Your Bidders

When someone bids on one of your items, you can always click on the bidder's name and check their feedback profile. There, you will see a section that shows how many bid retractions they've had in past transactions. You typically want to stay as far away as possible from members with high bid retraction levels. You can't very well kick a bidder off your auction without being certain but you can warn eBay ahead of time that there may be trouble brewing on the horizon.

eBay's Retraction Rules

The following is an excerpt from eBay's help file on retracting bids.

> *Timing Matters*
>
> *There are special rules about retracting bids, depending on when you originally placed the bid.*
>
> *If you place a bid before the last 12-hours of the listing: You may retract that bid before that last 12-hours, if your situation meets the above description of exceptional circumstances. You will not be allowed to retract that bid during the last 12-hours of the listing.*

When you retract a bid before the last 12 hours of a listing: you will eliminate all bids you have placed on that item. If you are correcting a bidding error, you will have to bid again.

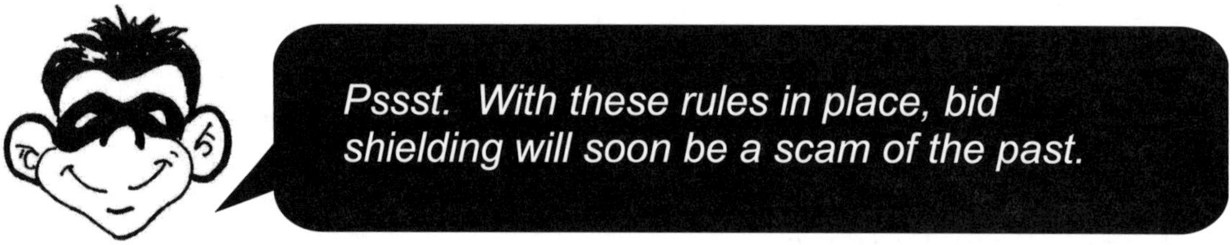

If you place a bid during the last 12-hours of the listing: You may retract the bid only within one hour after placing the bid (and if your situation meets eBay's exceptional circumstances description).

When you retract a bid within the last 12 hours of the listing: You will eliminate only the most recent bid you placed. Bids you placed prior to the last 12 hours will not be retracted.

If you are not allowed to retract your bid during the last 12-hours of the listing, you may contact the seller to request that your bid be canceled. The seller will have the discretion whether to cancel your bid.

ScamMaster I.Q. Review

Knowledge is power in the war on scammers. Here is your chance to test your scam I.Q. against the master himself; ScamMan.

Questions

1. What is a bid retraction on eBay?

2. Is a typo in a bid amount a valid reason for a bid retraction?

3. How can you check how many bid retractions a member has?

4. What are the retraction rules for a bid placed *before* the last 12-hours of a listing?

5. What are the retraction rules for a bid placed *during* the last 12-hours of a listing?

Answers

1. eBay allows, under very exceptional circumstances, bidders to retract a bid they submitted on a listing on eBay. 2. Yes. 3. You can check by visiting a member's feedback forum. 4. You may retract that bid before that last 12-hours, if your situation meets the description of exceptional circumstances. 5. If you place a bid during the last 12-hours of the listing: You may retract the bid only within one hour after placing the bid (and if your situation meets eBay's exceptional circumstances description).

eBay Scams Presents

THE ADVENTURES OF

SCAMMAN

CHAPTER 22

Electronics for Free Scam

Electronics for Free Scam

Everyone loves electronics these days! Everyone also knows how expensive these items can be. Not anymore! Imagine - TVs, Stereos, MP3 players, VCRs, DVDs and computers – all for free! "How?", you ask? There has to be a catch…" You better believe there is. You might want to pull up a chair for this one.

Scam Synopsis

Scammers are selling an information "Program" where, if followed properly, users will receive all their electronics for free. The "Program" asks users to fraudulently pretend they are a business and then solicit other companies for free goods.

1. ScamMan designs a very simple listing on eBay selling an information "Program". This program promises that if followed properly, users will be able to get all their electronics for free. He lists the "Program" at a starting bid price of $9.99.

Pssst. Some sellers will even go as far as setting a reserve price for their auction. A reserve price misleads bidders into thinking that the item holds some true value. Don't fall for it. Any way it's listed – it's a scam.

2. Intrigued bidders begin bidding on this item.

3. Eventually, a bidder wins the auction for the information "Program".

4. The bidder sends his/her payment through to ScamMan.

SCAM FLOW

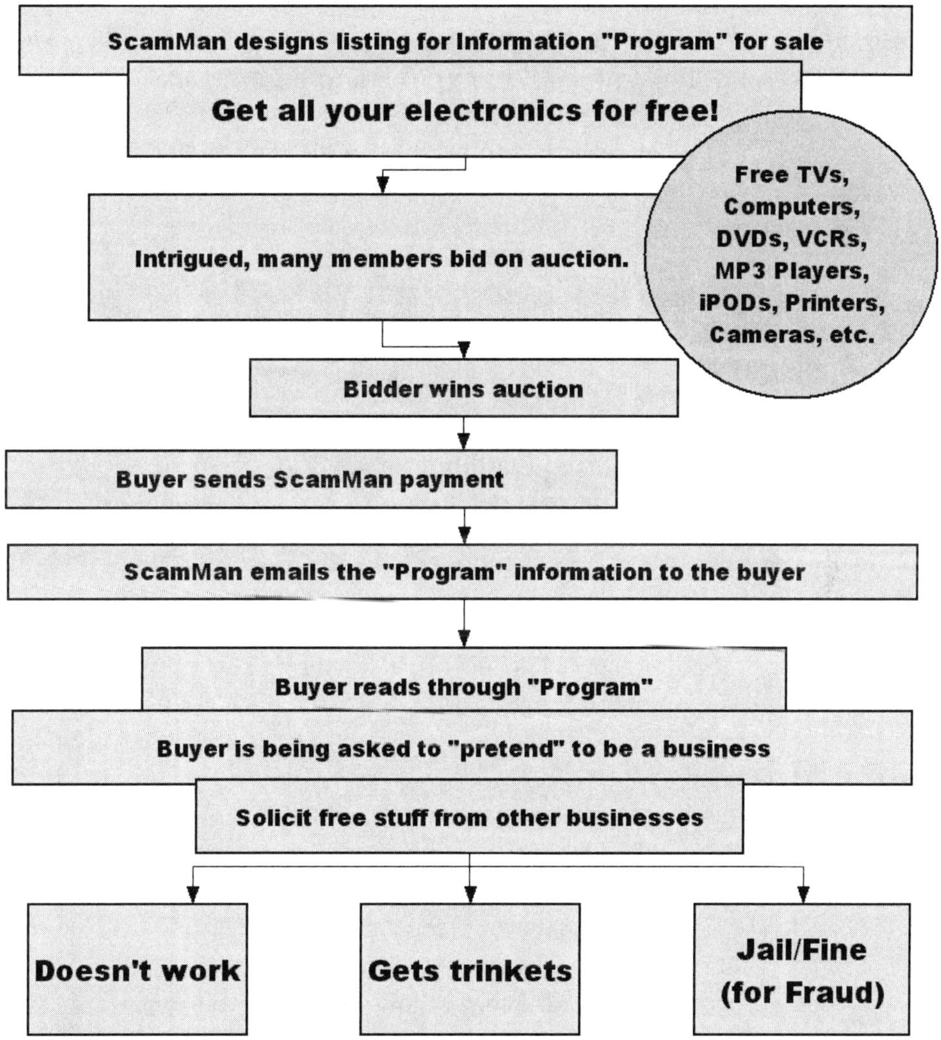
ScamMan designs listing for Information "Program" for sale
Get all your electronics for free!
Free TVs, Computers, DVDs, VCRs, MP3 Players, iPODs, Printers, Cameras, etc.
Intrigued, many members bid on auction.
Bidder wins auction
Buyer sends ScamMan payment
ScamMan emails the "Program" information to the buyer
Buyer reads through "Program"
Buyer is being asked to "pretend" to be a business
Solicit free stuff from other businesses
Doesn't work
Gets trinkets
Jail/Fine (for Fraud)

5. Upon receiving payment, ScamMan emails the information "Program" to the buyer.

6. The buyer receives the email and "Program" and reads through it.

The Actual Program Explained

The following text is the actual content of the "Program" sent to the buyer. That's right. At no cost I am providing you this information. Why am I being so generous? Because – it's a scam and you need to save your money. Don't be fooled by the words you'll read.

Pssst. This is my disclaimer to say – I am not encouraging anyone to follow the steps listed below. After reading through this document, it's going to sound really tempting but don't be fooled. It's a scam! It's illegal. Fraud is illegal. I am reproducing a similar "Program" so that you can see exactly how illegal it really is. Bottom line – not only is it illegal – it doesn't work.

How You Can Receive Consumer Electronics and Other Products Completely Free!

Introduction

First off I would like to thank you for purchasing my program and in the near future you will most likely be thanking yourself for purchasing it also. I would suggest getting comfortable because once you get started you won't want to stop. I know you are extremely anxious to know what exactly this bizarre sounding program is and how it works; now I am going to finally reveal this little known secret to you.

Getting Started

Please read everything over before you begin

STEP 1:

As I mentioned the only things you need to get started are a mailing address such as your house or apartment, and an email address. I'm assuming you already have a house or apartment, but if for some reason you don't you will need to get a post office box at a Mail Boxes Etc. or related service since some of your packages may require a signature upon delivery and they will sign on your behalf. Second you need an email address. You already have one since you received these files however I suggest setting up a second email account for business use. Your second email should be professional sounding; for example, something like "redwingsfan02@porn.com" wouldn't cut it. I would recommend the initial of your first name followed by your last name. If your name was John Smith, then "jsmith@email.com" would be great. A few good locations to get free email I have listed below. I wouldn't suggest getting an email at Hotmail or Yahoo considering literally any username you can think of is taken and they are well-known for being used to spam.

<Free email web addresses have been omitted to protect the innocent>

I also suggest opening up a free account with FedEx or DHL online using a debit or credit card. You will then be issued an account number. If you are unfamiliar with the way this service works, think of it as a credit card for shipping. You can include this account number with the emails you send. If the manufacturer requires you to pay for shipping, they can simply enter your account # on the international airwaybill for the package. The shipping costs are then billed to the credit or debit card on your account. You do not want to have these packages shipped overnight or 2 day airmail. As you can imagine a TV sent FedEx overnight from Malaysia to the US is not too frugal. Instead, check with the shipping courier your account is with (FedEx, DHL) by phone to speak with customer service and find out which international shipping method would be the absolute cheapest. DHL in most cases is the cheapest since they offer slower delivery than FedEx. Once you have researched and found which shipping method is cheapest (each courier has names, i.e. "FedEx International Economy Rate) mention in the email you would like the sample shipped using that method. Although paying for shipping is not necessary to receive free products, you should have much better success if you do. The cost of the sample usually isn't what the manufacturer cares about; it is the cost of shipping.

STEP 2:

Now that you have the two things necessary you can start. Instead of you searching and seeking out companies and their products directly, I am going to provide you with a website which will allow you to do it directly to begin with, which my company as well as hundreds of thousands of others uses. Eventually after you have done this for a while you will be able to search out other manufacturers directly to contact using search engines. However this website offers access to about 150,000 suppliers which are plenty to get started with.

<Website address has been removed to protect the innocent.>

After you arrive at the website you will want to register for a membership, which is free. Click on the "Login/Register" and you will come to a page for current members to enter their login name and password, scroll below to where it says "register now." Now that you will be conducting business relations you will need to have a name for your company. Once you have decided enter the name as well as the rest of your other contact information and submit. Then select the categories of items you are interested in if you would like to receive product alerts (optional).

Now you are ready to begin. On the main page of the Global Sources website, click on "product search" and from there you can either browse or search. Take an hour or so to relax and look around at products which interest you. Do not contact or request any samples yet.

STEP 3:

Now that you have looked over the products it is time to start requesting your free samples. Since you are just starting, you should begin with products (from any category) that have a consumer retail value of $20 or less. Only after you have had some experience and received a few should you start requesting the more costly items such as televisions, DVD players, etc.

There are a couple ways you can contact the companies to receive your samples. Once you are on the page of a single specific product, you can click on the company's name near the top (it should be in a blue font) which will take you to a page which will have their contact information including at least one or two email addresses. You can then email them from your email address.

Another way to email them is to click on "request sample" or "inquire now" on the product's page; this will contact the companies through the Global Sources website instead of you emailing them directly.

When you email the companies, you should introduce yourself, mention you are interested in their product(s) and you would like them to send you more information regarding the product(s) as well as a sample unit. Be sure to include your mailing address. I have enclosed a picture of an actual sample correspondence between myself and a company (must censor text: company policy). What you write in your letter is up to you, it does not have to be long; a paragraph or so may do. The information contained in my letter is true; I do not advocate or support you writing any type of fictional information in your correspondences. Include your DHL or FedEx account number as well as the shipping method you would like if you opened an account.

STEP 4:

You may have to communicate by email with the companies a couple times back and fourth after your initial request. One thing I cannot stress enough is to be patient. In the United States, we do everything fast with a "gotta be done now, can't wait" attitude and adhere to a strict schedule. Many other parts of the world including much of Asia are not like this. You may not receive a reply to your email for a few weeks. This does not mean they are ignoring you, that is just the way business is conducted there and they reply just as slowly to large corporations usually also.

When you do receive your free products, they will usually be shipped as a "commercial sample, no value" so you do not pay any tariffs on them. This is a very good thing; tariffs can be almost 40% of the product's value! Below is a picture of an actual invoice.

TIPS AND TRICKS:

(1) Remember there is no limit to how many different manufactures you can request samples from; the more you contact, the more free products you will receive.

(2) Start out small by requesting low valued items (products with a retail value of <$20) this allows you to gain the experience you need. It is very important you follow this step.

(3) Contact companies which do not have any of their products pictured. Click on the "view more suppliers" when you have come to the last page of the pictured products in a

category. Email them and have them forward you their product brochures first.

(4) If you pay shipping costs you will have greater success.

(5) Be patient.

(6) After you are experienced you can begin contacting manufacturers not listed on Global Sources by locating them using search engines such as Yahoo.

(7) If there is a specific model you must have, and the company does not give out free samples, you can always purchase one or more at true wholesale cost.

(8) Remember if you receive a product you don't particularly like you can always sell them.

GOOD LUCK AND HAVE FUN!

7. After reading through the document, the buyer decides to give it a whirl.

8. The results are sometimes mixed. They can range from:

- Buyer receives nothing
- Buyer receives some small trinkets, i.e. pens, key chains, etc.
- Buyer is fined or jailed for fraud

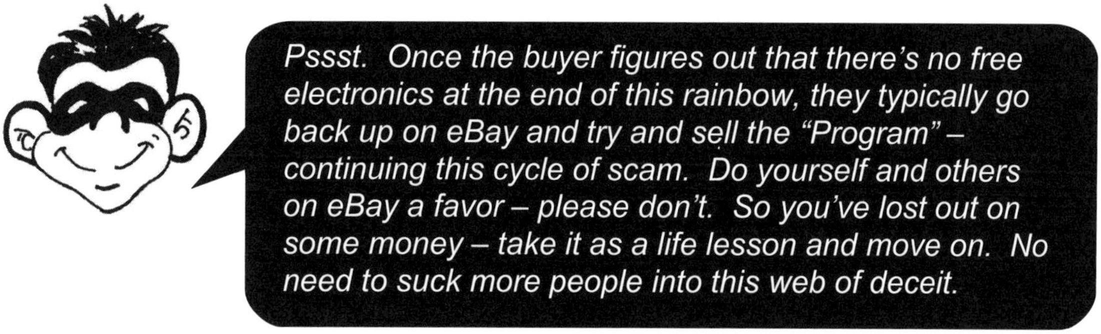

Best Defense

This is a very popular scam so don't get caught in the hype, protect yourself by following these defenses.

Are There Others?

For auctions like these, always check to see if anyone else is selling the same thing. In this case, I did a search on "free electronics" and my computer almost went on the fritz it was so overloaded. This is a popular scam and if there's this many people attempting to sell it, then it can't be that big of a secret – right?

Get Rich Quick

They don't work. There is no easy way to make lots of money, lose 200 pounds or in this case get something expensive for free. Avoid these types of auctions. They're either lies, illegal or both.

Ask

If you are still not convinced that all these types of listings are scams – ask the seller if it's the same "Program" shown in this chapter. If it is, then you are being encouraged to lie, pretend to be someone you're not, spam, and commit fraud. I will leave it to you and your conscience on how you'd like to proceed.

ScamMaster I.Q. Review

Knowledge is power in the war on scammers. Here is your chance to test your scam I.Q. against the master himself; ScamMan.

Questions

1. How is the "program" typically sent out to buyers?

2. Name at least two illegal practices contained in this "program".

3. Name two of the three potential outcomes for a buyer running this program.

4. What does a scammed buyer typically do when they find out this program doesn't work?

5. Why would searching on eBay for the same "program" help in averting this scam?

Answers

1. By email only. 2. Fraud (impersonating a business), spam and lying. 3. Buyer receives nothing, buyer receives some small trinkets, (i.e. pens, key chains, etc.), Buyer is fined or jailed for fraud. 4. They list the "program" and try and recoup their lost money. 5. Finding hundreds of others selling the same program is a good indicator of a secret program that isn't much of a secret.

eBay Scams Presents

THE ADVENTURES OF

SCAMMAN

CHAPTER 23

MIA Scam

MIA Scam

It's your word against theirs. It's as simple as that. Did you send the package? Of course you did. Did the shipping company ship it properly? Of course they did. Did the buyer receive the item. Of course he did. Unfortunately, the buyer's version of the events is a little different. Let's read on.

Scam Synopsis

Buyer receives item and then claims it never arrived. It's as simple as that.

1. ScamMan scours eBay looking for low cost items he wants (i.e. DVDs, CDs, books, etc.)

Pssst. The mark for this type of scam is typically (and I do mean typically) big wheeling sellers with lots of experience on eBay. They are usually the busiest dealing with sometimes several transactions a day.

2. Once he locates the item he wants, ScamMan bids to win.

3. During the bidding process, ScamMan endears himself to the seller with emails asking very polite and professional questions regarding the item. The following are the types of questions he would ask:

- Is the DVD the special edition version or the original release?
- Is this a first printing of the hard cover release or is it the second printing?
- What condition is the CD insert in?

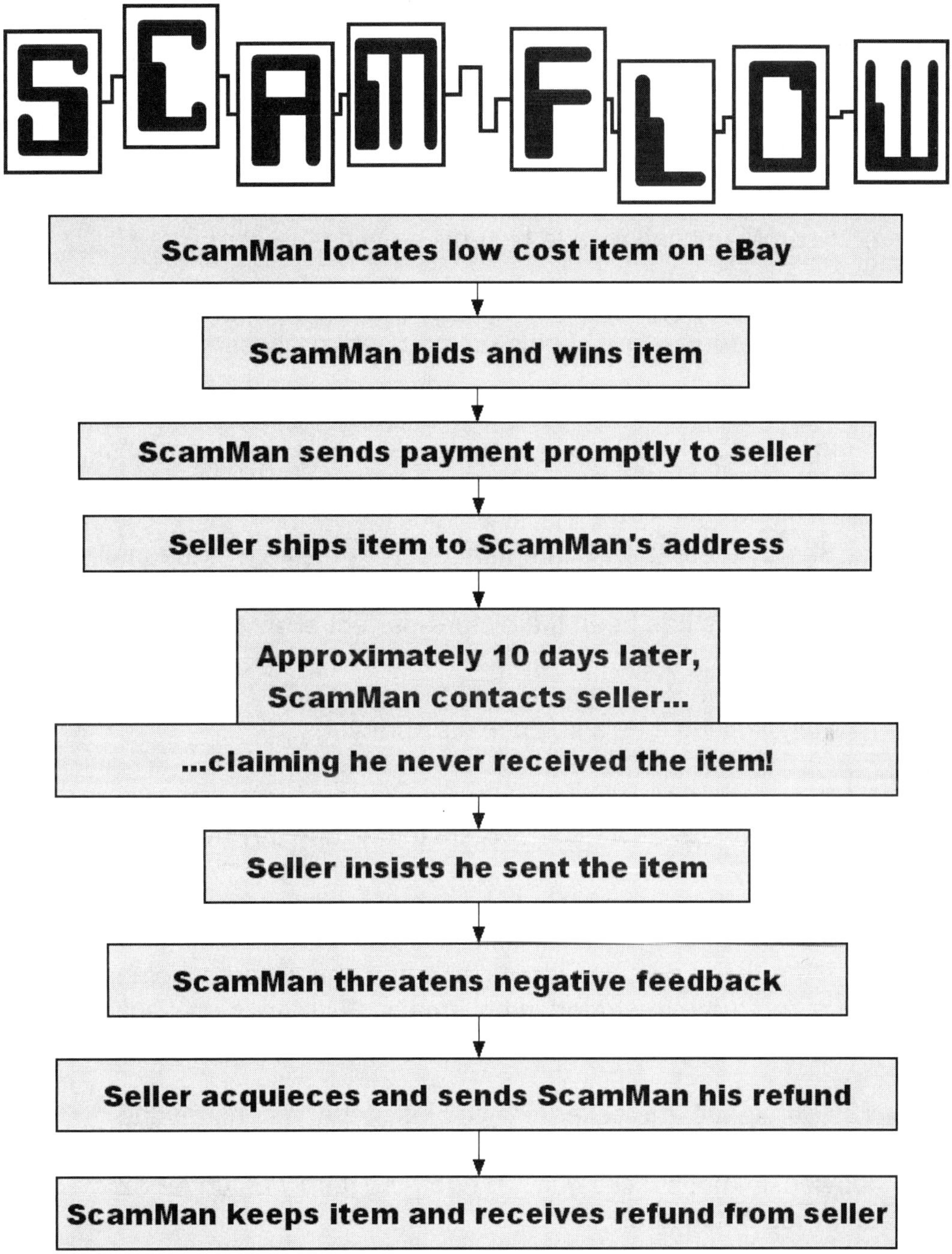
SCAM FLOW
ScamMan locates low cost item on eBay
ScamMan bids and wins item
ScamMan sends payment promptly to seller
Seller ships item to ScamMan's address
Approximately 10 days later, ScamMan contacts seller...
...claiming he never received the item!
Seller insists he sent the item
ScamMan threatens negative feedback
Seller acquieces and sends ScamMan his refund
ScamMan keeps item and receives refund from seller

Pssst. ScamMan's goal is to build a level of trust and credibility with the seller. By asking questions and being friendly, the seller is even more convinced that ScamMan is a legitimate bidder and potential buyer.

4. ScamMan continues to bid until he wins the item.

5. Very promptly, ScamMan contacts the seller with his shipping address and begins the payment process.

6. The seller is absolutely elated with the speed at which things are moving. Upon receiving payment, he too promptly ships out the item to ScamMan's address.

7. Shortly thereafter, ScamMan receives his item in the mail. The item is in perfect condition – exactly as advertised. Up until now, this has been the picture-perfect eBay transaction.

8. Around five days later, ScamMan contacts the seller (politely) asking if he's shipped his item yet.

9. Surprised, the seller explains that he has already shipped the item and assumes it should be there "any day now".

10. Snickering, ScamMan waits five more days.

11. ScamMan contacts the seller again, this time sounding more and more frustrated in his emails. "Where is my item?" he asks in his communications.

12. Perplexed, the seller retraces his steps, reconfirms the address and does what he can to locate the package. He is "obviously" not successful. To boot, the item was under $25 so it was not insured.

13. Acting furious, ScamMan contacts the seller threatening to leave negative feedback and contact eBay to report him.

14. Beaten, tired and extremely busy, the seller gives up and sends ScamMan his refund.

15. ScamMan calls up his buddy Scummy and invites him over to watch his new "free" DVD.

Best Defense

There are a variety of precautionary measures that you can take to avoid getting caught up in this scam.

Use Delivery Confirmation

The United States Postal Service's Delivery Confirmation (DC) is a service that allows sellers to confirm that a package has been delivered to a buyer location. This fee based service will give sellers access to the date and time of a delivery, zip code of where the shipment was delivered and any information about any attempted deliveries and forwarded or returned shipments. Using the DC is strongly recommended to all sellers.

Pssst. One of the biggest gripes against the DC is that it can only confirm delivery and not actual receipt by a person. This service does not require a signature therefore making it possible that the item went to the wrong person at the wrong address.

Check Feedback

This is more of a preventative strategy but nevertheless an important one. Always check a buyer's feedback. Do they have a record of "non-receipt" items? Are they constantly causing problems for sellers? If all the other sellers are anything like you, they probably backed down as well and refunded this member's money. That would mean they also didn't leave any negative feedback for fear of retribution. This is a classic case of feedback bullying.

Disclaimer

When all else fails – include a disclaimer in your listing. If you prefer to not accept refunds – state it. Some scammers will avoid your listings because they know there's no use trying. You can also list all the safeguards you use to ensure items are shipped responsibly, like insurance and the DC. For example:

Orders received and confirmed delivered by the United States Postal Service's Delivery Confirmation (DC) service.

Shipping Feedback

Last but not least, you can always stress in your listing how fantastic your feedback is with regards to shipping. This can further reinforce in a scammer's mind the steps you will always take to ensure proper delivery.

ScamMaster I.Q. Review

Knowledge is power in the war on scammers. Here is your chance to test your scam I.Q. against the master himself; ScamMan.

Questions

1. Which kind of sellers are typically targeted for this type of scam?

2. Why does the buyer's strategy involve building a rapport with the seller prior to running the scam?

3. What does DC stand for? How can it be used as a defense against this scam?

4. What are some limitations of the DC defense strategy?

5. How will checking a buyer's feedback help – as a preventative method?

Answers

1. Big wheeling, high feedback scores, seasoned eBay sellers. 2. By building a rapport, the seller is less likely to feel suspicious of the buyer during the course of the transaction, leading up to the scam. 3. The United States Postal Service's Delivery Confirmation (DC) is a service that allows sellers to confirm that a package has been delivered to a buyer location. 4. One of the biggest gripes against the DC is that it can only confirm delivery and not actual receipt by a person. This service does not require a signature therefore making it possible that the item went to the wrong person at the wrong address. 5. Do they have a record of "non-receipt" items? Are they constantly causing problems for sellers?

eBay Scams Presents

THE ADVENTURES OF

SCAMMAN

CHAPTER 24

Dictionary Attacks

Dictionary Attacks

If this scam doesn't make you think twice about your password, then I'm not sure what will. Believe it or not, there are still people out there using the following words as passwords: test, password, wife's name, husband's name, pet's name, company name. You're all walking targets. Listen to what I preach and I will save you all.

Scam Synopsis

Scammers use an automated program to find passwords of known eBay user IDs. These automated programs search through databases of common passwords and dictionaries of words.

1. ScamMan captures and stores thousands of eBay member's user IDs.

2. ScamMan scours the web looking for bots that perform dictionary attacks. These bots are automated programs that try to match user IDs with lists of common passwords and dictionary words.

3. ScamMan finds just the one he's looking for.

4. Running the bot, ScamMan strikes pay dirt and breaks into an innocent member's account. With the member's user ID and password, ScamMan has successfully hijacked this account.

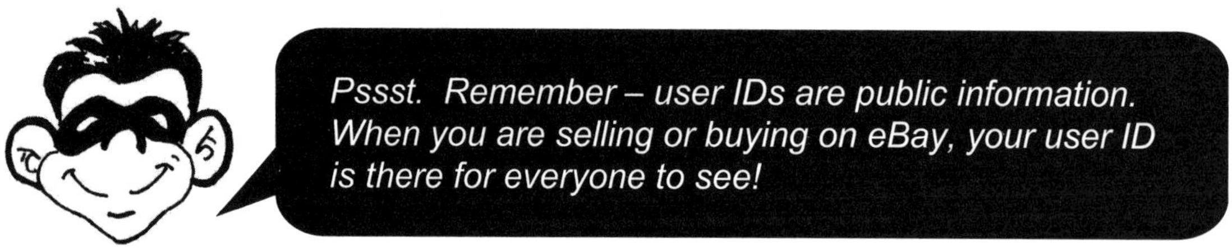

SCAM FLOW

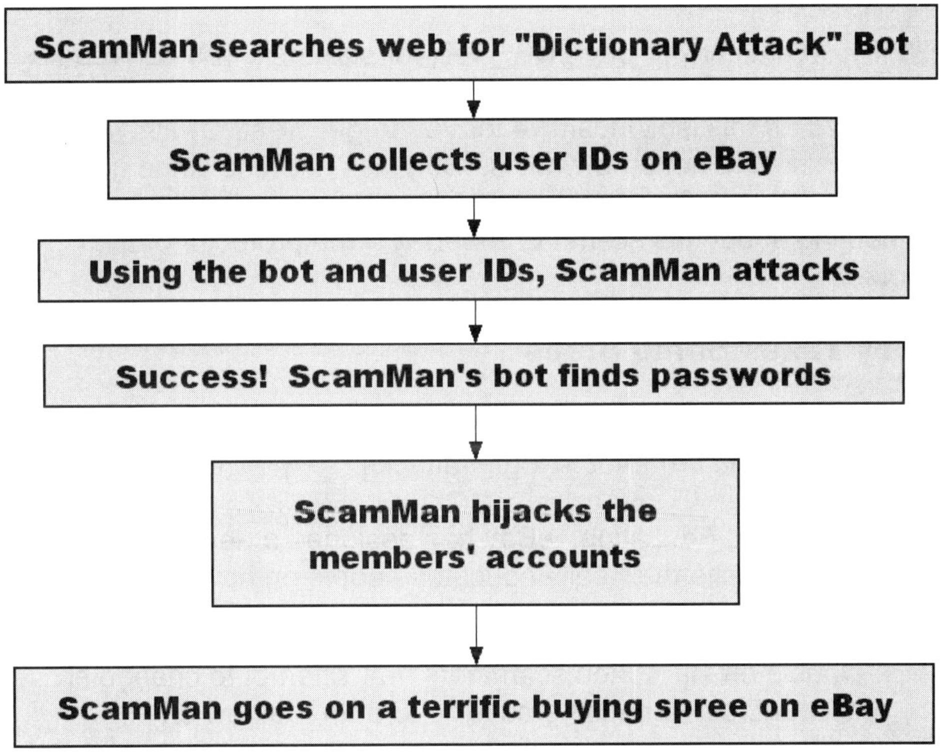
ScamMan searches web for "Dictionary Attack" Bot
ScamMan collects user IDs on eBay
Using the bot and user IDs, ScamMan attacks
Success! ScamMan's bot finds passwords
ScamMan hijacks the members' accounts
ScamMan goes on a terrific buying spree on eBay

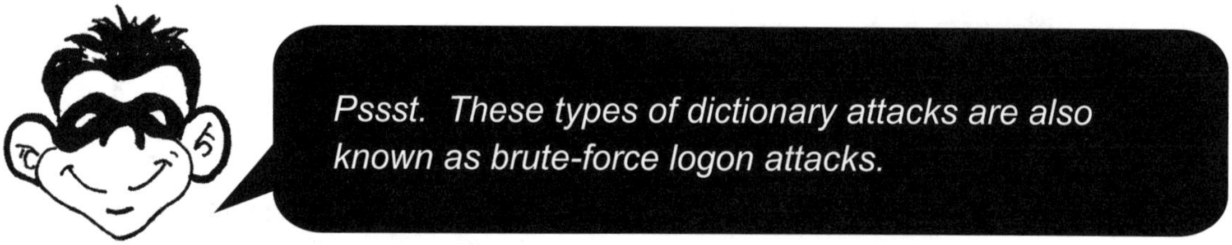

5. ScamMan goes on a terrific buying spree using this new found user ID and password.

Best Defense

Oh my. What can we do now? Well, for starters – you can read one of the early chapters in this book on how to create a proper password. If this isn't incentive for you to get creative with your passwords – I'm not sure what is. But, alas, there is some good news in all this. eBay has risen to the occasion and done something about this scam. Enter eBay – the protector of the people!

eBay Takes Some Steps

Here are some of the steps eBay has taken to overcome this issue of dictionary and brute-force logon attacks:

- Password Education. eBay has designed a new page on their website that really educates people on how to create the best and most secure passwords.
- Double email. When scammers now attempt to change an account, confirmation emails go to both the new email address as well as the old.
- Limited Attempts. After a certain number of "attempted" logins, a member (or scammer) will be rerouted to a password information screen. There, they will be asked to punch in a

security code that is actually an image. Bots cannot read images. Humans can. This fix alone should render this scam extinct and put a lot of bot creators out of business.

ScamMaster I.Q. Review

Knowledge is power in the war on scammers. Here is your chance to test your scam I.Q. against the master himself; ScamMan.

Questions

1. How can you easily get a member's email address on eBay?

2. What is a bot?

3. What are Dictionary Attacks also known as?

4. Tell me about eBay's prevention fixes for this problem? Name two of the three.

5. What happens on a scammer's third attempt to brute-force logon a member's account?

Answers

1. Two ways: Ask the seller a question link, and await their reply OR Contact Seller link, and await their reply. 2. A program designed to search for information on the Internet with little human intervention. 3. Brute-force logon attacks. 4. Limited Attempts, Double email – both your new email address and old, Password Education. 5. Bots will be asked to punch in a security code that they have to read off of an image. Bots cannot read images.

eBay Scams Presents

THE ADVENTURES OF

SCAMMAN

CHAPTER 25

Check the Big Checks

Check the Big Checks

Everyone loves getting big checks – especially if they're made out for more than you expected. Unfortunately, when this happens on eBay, you're most likely about to fall for a scam that's been around since 1989. A big check on eBay typically means big trouble for a seller. The warning signs are clear so you shouldn't have too much of a problem keeping this one at bay. Enough chatter - let's get to it.

Scam Synopsis

Scammer wins auction and sends seller a cashier's check for more than the amount of what they are purchasing. The seller is asked to return the difference. By the time the check clears and is discovered to be a phony, the seller has already sent the difference through to the scammer – never to be seen again.

1. ScamMan goes to the bank and gets himself a legitimate cashier's check.

2. Using his scanner, ScamMan scans the cashier's check into his computer for later use.

3. ScamMan roams the auctions on eBay looking for his next target. He finds someone selling a car for $5000.

4. Using the Buy It Now feature, ScamMan purchases the car at $5000.

5. ScamMan contacts the seller letting him know how excited he is, and that he will be paying by cashier's check (one of the seller's approved methods of payment).

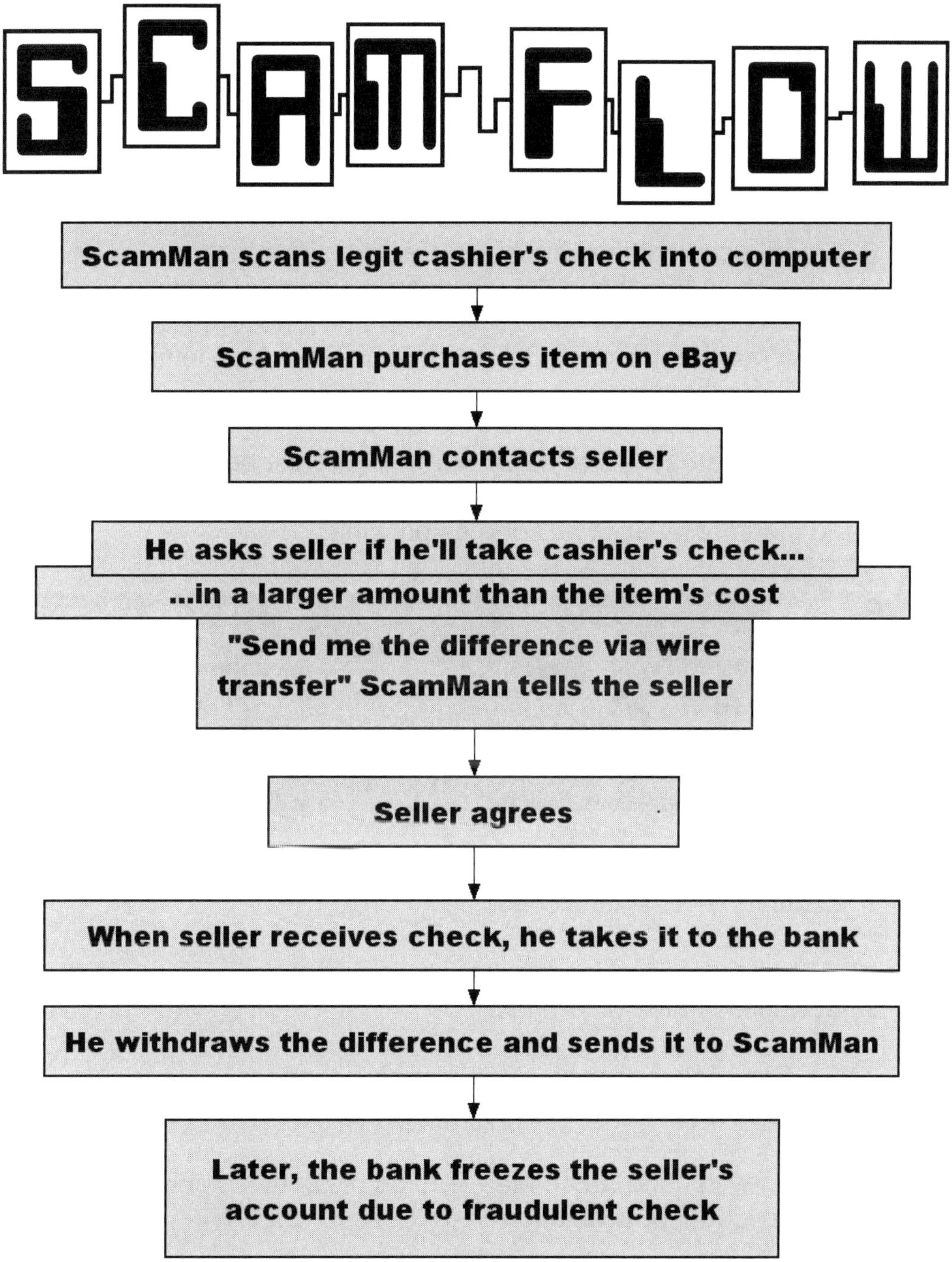
SCAM FLOW
ScamMan scans legit cashier's check into computer
ScamMan purchases item on eBay
ScamMan contacts seller
He asks seller if he'll take cashier's check...
...in a larger amount than the item's cost
"Send me the difference via wire transfer" ScamMan tells the seller
Seller agrees
When seller receives check, he takes it to the bank
He withdraws the difference and sends it to ScamMan
Later, the bank freezes the seller's account due to fraudulent check

6. Back at his computer, ScamMan modifies the scanned image of the cashier check to be made payable to the Seller for the amount of $8000. He prints the check from his high-end printer.

7. ScamMan sends the Seller the phony check.

8. Upon receipt of the check, the Seller notices that the check is actually made out for a lot more money than he expected.

9. The "good Samaritan" Seller contacts ScamMan letting him know about the error.

10. ScamMan asks that he send the difference back to him via wire transfer preferably. He's is a big hurry and he will need that money back as soon as possible.

Pssst. Usually the excuse used is something family or death related. For example, ScamMan will tell the seller he needs the difference sent back to him immediately because his mother is dying in a hospital in another country.

11. The soon-to-be duped seller runs to the bank, deposits the counterfeit cashier's check.

12. The bank holds the check for a couple of days. The seller then withdraws the difference.

13. Off the seller goes to a wire transfer center where he quickly sends the difference to ScamMan.

14. Money in hand, ScamMan puts on his beach clothes and heads to Cuba for a vacation.

15. Meanwhile, the buyer has been contacted by his bank and told the cashier's check was fraudulent. His bank account is frozen until the money can be repaid. The seller now owes his bank $3000 plus several service and penalty fees.

This scam can take many forms. Here is another variation.

1. ScamMan goes to the bank and gets himself a legitimate cashier's check.

2. Using his scanner, ScamMan scans the cashier's check into his computer for later use.

3. ScamMan roams the auctions on eBay looking for his next target. He finds someone selling a car for $5000.

4. Using the Buy It Now feature, ScamMan purchases the car at $5000.

Here's where the scam takes a turn from the previous example. Instead of sending the higher priced check "by accident", ScamMan does the following:

5. ScamMan contacts the seller with a very sad story of hardship in his native country. He explains that he has several large checks that he cannot cash due to political reasons in his own country. He asks if he could send the seller a check for $10,000 instead. All he asks is that the seller return to him the difference, minus $250 reward for helping him with his plight.

6. Feeling sad, the seller agrees to this phony story and awaits the check.

7. Back at his computer, ScamMan modifies the scanned image of the cashier check to be made payable to the Seller for the amount of $10,000. He prints the check from his high-end printer.

8. ScamMan sends the Seller the phony check,

9. ScamMan asks that he send the difference back to him via wire transfer preferably.

10. The soon-to-be duped seller runs to the bank, deposits the counterfeit cashier's check.

11. The bank holds the check for a couple of days. The seller then withdraws the difference.

12. The seller goes to a wire transfer center where he quickly sends the difference to ScamMan.

13. Money in hand, ScamMan puts on his beach clothes and heads to Cuba for a vacation.

14. Meanwhile, the buyer has been contacted by his bank and told the cashier's check was fraudulent. His bank account is frozen until the money can be repaid. The seller now owes his bank $5000 plus several service and penalty fees.

There are several other variations as well that are worth noting:

- The Scammer sends a cashier's check for a much larger amount to cover "unknown" shipping and other costs. They ask for return payment for the difference.

- "Very Urgent Business Proposal" and need your help transferring millions of dollars from a secret account in Africa to yours in America.
- Scammer tells the seller that he has a "friend" in the United States who owes him money. He explains that this friend will send the seller a cashier's check, but the check will be a lot higher than the item costs.

Here's an example of the type of communication you would receive from someone using this scam format:

From: ScamMan (scamman@scammers.com)

Sent: Sunday, January 11th, 2004 6:32 PM

To: Unsuspecting, innocent seller,

Subject: Paying and Shippping

I am someone who does purchasing and supply and live in Belgium. I have people I work with in USofA and they owe me money through other dealings. They are ready to pay me by check but the amount owing much more than the price of the item I've bought off of you.

I will ask my American friend to send you the check anyway and I expect you will send the balance to my shipping agent.

My shipping agent will contact you for the pick up after the transaction must have been completed.

Give me your address and I will make sure the check is sent fastly.

Sincerely

ScamMan

- The Seller receives a letter from a "government official" or businessman in Nigeria speaking in confidence about a large sum of cash that is available. The scammer then states that if the seller helps with the transfer, they can share in the profits.

- A lot of these scams actually involve classified ads for "check cashing" jobs. The people who reply to these ads are then sent large checks that they are asked to deposit. Once deposited, these people are asked to quickly wire the money via wire transfer services. The outcome is always the same – checks are fraudulent.

Best Defense

There are several telltale signs of this scam in action. In fact, most of the scammers pulling this scam typically follow the same MO. Pay heed to these signs, they may save you a lot of money.

Google It

I've said it once, and I'll say it ten more times. Google is the way to go. If you feel you may be falling victim to a scam, go to Google and punch the details in. You'll be surprised at all the results that will most likely pop up. I couldn't believe how popular it really was until Google told me so – over 150 hits.

Three's a Crowd

Typically, when dealing on eBay, the transactions are between a seller and buyer. They are not between a seller, middleman and buyer. Avoid those dealings where there's an additional person involved in the mix. Those almost always spell T-R-O-U-B-L-E.

Payment Method

These days, no payment method is really 100% safe but some are definitely safer than others. If you get any request from a buyer to pay by cashier's check, you most likely have a scammer waiting to scam. Refuse and run the other way.

More is Less

Beware of anyone offering you more money than you asked for. If the item was purchased at $500 and the buyer wants to send you $1000 – warning bells should ring in your head. This is scam. Stay away.

Wired

Not much to say here but the following: Avoid wire transfer services when dealing on eBay – unless you know the other person (really well) on the other end. Wire transfers are the preferred payment method of choice for scammers worldwide.

Overseas

Be really skeptical of any overseas offers from strangers. They are almost always frauds in disguise.

Clear the Check First

If for whatever reason you accept cashier's checks as viable method of payment, always contact the bank that issued it. Your primary goal is to ensure it has been authorized and that everything is on the up and up.

Too Polite

Believe it or not, one telltale sign that I'm being scammed is when a buyer is far too polite in their written communications. If I count more than ten "pleases" in an email, I know something's fishy in the state of eBay. Obviously, this isn't enough to really accuse anyone of anything – on its own. Coupled with some of the other things mentioned in this section though - who knows?

Doctor, Doctor

Many of the scammers who pull this stunt identify themselves as doctors or even reverends in some cases. In my world, doctors and reverends can almost always spell. Keep your eye on the spelling and grammar issues. These too can be signs that you're about to be scammed.

Yahoo! or Hotmail

Many times these individuals will be emailing you claiming to be part of a large organization. Check their email address. If it's a Yahoo! or Hotmail account, you're most likely not dealing with who you think you are. Scam Alert!

Money First

If the correspondence back and fourth with this buyer seems to be more focused on the payment side rather than the actual item or shipping, you may be in the midst of a scammer.

ScamMaster I.Q. Review

Knowledge is power in the war on scammers. Here is your chance to test your scam I.Q. against the master himself; ScamMan.

Questions

1. What are some of the ways a scammer can encourage a seller to send them the "difference" as quickly as possible?

2. What is a "check-cashing" job?

3. How can Google help in preventing this scam?

4. Why are Yahoo! and Hotmail email accounts potentially a red flag for this scam?

5. What is the most obvious sign that you are getting duped by this scam?

Answers

1. Death in the family, wife in hospital, any family emergency. 2. The people who reply these ads are sent large checks that they are asked to deposit. Once deposited, these people are asked to quickly wire the money via wire transfer services. The outcome is always the same – checks are fraudulent. 3. Look up any scam on Google to see how popular it is. 4. No legitimate business will send emails using a Yahoo! or Hotmail account. 5. Scammer sends you a check that in an amount larger than the actual price of the item.

eBay Scams Presents

THE ADVENTURES OF

SCAMMAN

CHAPTER 26

Help Wanted Scam

Help Wanted Scam

All of us have been in positions where we either hate the jobs we have or worse, don't have a job at all. Enter the Help Wanted Scam! Preying on people like you and me, along comes the perfect job: big money, exciting and quick returns . Now that's a great combination. Too good to be true? You better believe it is. Let's find out why.

Scam Synopsis

Con artists in Europe are using job listing sites to lure potential job-seekers into an eBay scam. The employment position posted is usually for a sales related job selling electronics in the United States. If the sales rep sells an item, the con artists promise to deliver from Europe - once they receive payment via wire transfer. The sales representative collects payment from the buyer and sends it through to the con men who in turn send nothing and disappear.

1. ScamMan puts together a help wanted ad for a career site in the United States. A representation of this ad appears on the following pages. The position posted is really exciting with huge opportunities for growth, large cash potential and quick turnarounds. This is the perfect job. All you really need is an eBay account and a great feedback record.

2. eBay members who meet this criteria contact the employer and proceed through a very brief interview process – all by email. The employer explains the position in the following way:

SCAM FLOW
ScamMan creates help wanted ad and posts it
Employer
eBay member applies and gets the job
Employee
eBay member lists ScamMan's item(s) for sale
Buyers bid and ultimately win auctions
eBay member collects payment for items from buyers and deposits in his bank
Employee
eBay member wires cash to ScamMan
Employee
Employer
ScamMan receives cash, does not ship item and disappears
Employer
eBay member left to deal with angry buyers
Employee
eBay member reported, suspended and jailed

> Hello Potential Candidate,
>
> My name is (name) and I will be your contact from this point forward for this position.
>
> We are new to the U.S. market and are in the process of opening a U.S. bank account. As we cut through all the red tape getting our systems in place, we have an immediate need for a sales executive in the U.S. who can make things happen. We are in the business of electronics and can sell them at next to wholesale prices. We are asking our sales executive to sell our electronics on eBay and share in the profits with our organization. If you successfully sell at least one of our items each month, we will pay you a monthly salary of $1500. We will take care of all shipping from our native country, free of charge. Until we are set up in the U.S. with a bank account, we request you wire all payments to our account here in Eastern Europe. If this position with our organization seems like a good fit for you, please let us know as soon as possible.
>
> Thanks for reading,
>
> Signature

3. Intrigued by this offer, many members respond to the email seeking the role.

4. The Scammers on the other end of this con provide the members with all the information they need by email. This typically includes electronic photos of the different items for sale, system specifications, and pricing. These scammers are extremely professional in their communications with these members.

5. “Victim” members began their listing process. Taking the information they have, they list these electronics items on eBay using their user IDs and accounts.

6. Items are purposely priced to sell with very low opening bid prices. This attracts the most amounts of buyers sometimes creating a bidding frenzy.

Electro-SCAM©

Detailed Employment Offer

EMPLOYMENT OFFER

Company name: Electro-SCAM®

Position Required: Sales Executive (eBay)

- **Location:** North America (preferably USA)
- **Position Type:** Contract
- **Field:** Sales
- **Main Role:** Selling wholesale electronics

Description of company :

We are an Eastern European wholesaler of electronic goods. We are currently going through the process of starting our U.S. operations and require sales executives who can assist by selling our products online.

Position description:
You are an experienced eBayer with at least 2 years selling power. You have ten or more feedback points and are well respected in your eBay circles. You have a knack for selling and love dealing with clients. No selling experience necessary.

Rates are negotiable but extremely attractive. Pay will be distributed on a monthly basis.

WANT TO APPLY?

- **By Internet:**
- Send all communications to scamming@scammer.com

Help Wanted “Scam” Ad

7. As their auctions come to a close, these unsuspecting sellers (now working for this “organization”) are joyous as they make sale after sale.

8. Each seller contacts their buyer requesting payment for the item they’ve purchased.

9. Upon receiving payment, the seller deposits the funds into their bank account. From there, they withdraw the equivalent in cash.

10. From a wire transfer center, the seller wires the cash to their contact in Eastern Europe.

11. Their contact at the organization confirms receipt of the cash and promises delivery by a certain date for the buyer.

12. The seller contacts the buyer with the information regarding shipping dates.

13. In the meantime, the seller is encouraged to continue selling these electronics online.

14. The cycle continues with each seller successfully selling two to three items within a two week period.

15. Eventually, buyers began contacting their sellers wondering where their items are.

16. The sellers contact their supplier in Eastern Europe looking for support.

17. Their Eastern European employer provides them with excuses that seem feasible and provide new shipping dates for their buyers.

18. Again, the sellers are encouraged to continue selling. More sales are made and more cash is wired.

19. Finally, buyers can wait no longer and they leave negative feedback for the sellers and report them to the authorities and eBay.

20. The sellers frantically contact their "employer" in Eastern Europe looking for answers.

21. The organization never existed and the scammers have completely disappeared leaving their "employees" out in the cold to deal with these matters on their own.

Pssst. Similar scams have occurred where the international "organization" has requested eBay auction payments be collected through an "employee's" PayPal account. Same scam – different color.

Best Defense

If it sounds too good to be true – it probably is. How many times will I have to say that in this book? I imagine probably ten more times. The following is advice on how to best protect yourself against this scam:

Avoid Wires

The problem with wire transfers is that they are pretty much untraceable. If you don't know the person on the other end of the wire – you're most likely not going to see that cash ever again. Avoid the wire. Avoid the wire. Avoid the wire. Get it?

International

It's difficult to say that you shouldn't deal with anyone who lives outside of North America but I can say that you should exercise more caution when you do. Many of the laws that protect us here do not apply to our international counterparts - making their countries a potential hotbed of scamming activity. Be careful and where possible – deal at home.

Too Personal

Didn't your mommy ever tell you to never talk to strangers? Then why do we do it all the time and act surprised when we get ripped off? No one and I mean no one should ever get access to your personal information like credit card numbers, social insurance, bank accounts and addresses.

Verify

Always insist on contact information you can verify, i.e. phone numbers, etc. In the case of this scam, never agree to work for an employer you can't verify using systems similar to the Better Business Bureau. If they plan to pay you and you plan to collect, they should be a legitimate business – and willing to prove it.

ScamMaster I.Q. Review

Knowledge is power in the war on scammers. Here is your chance to test your scam I.Q. against the master himself; ScamMan.

Questions

1. Where are the scammer's help wanted ads typically posted?

2. Which payment method is the seller required to use when paying their "employer organization"?

3. Why is it important that only applicants with eBay accounts and high feedback scores apply for this scam to be effective?

4. Why is dealing with international customers/organizations riskier than dealing in North America.

5. Name two ways an eBay member could avert this scam?

Answers

1. Job listing sites, career boards, want ads in newspapers, etc. 2. Wire transfers 3. These members would be credible and trusted in the eBay community. They are more apt to sell big ticket items. 4. International laws are different than in North America. 5. Avoid Wire Transfers, avoid international dealings, never give away your personal information, verify all businesses.

eBay Scams Presents

THE ADVENTURES OF

SCAMMAN

CHAPTER 27

Grow Your Own Escrow

Grow your Own Escrow

Leave it to scammers to wreck a really good thing. Escrows were put in place to make buyers and sellers feel more confident and secure in their transactions. With a third party acting as the "middle person" – how could anything go wrong? Just watch.

Scam Synopsis

Scammers convince buyers to send payment via a fake escrow service. The fake escrow service is owned and run by the scammer. The fraudsters collect the payment and disappear.

1. ScamMan creates his own escrow website called "Es-Crown Services". He patterns it after eBay's recommended and legitimate choice – escrow.com.

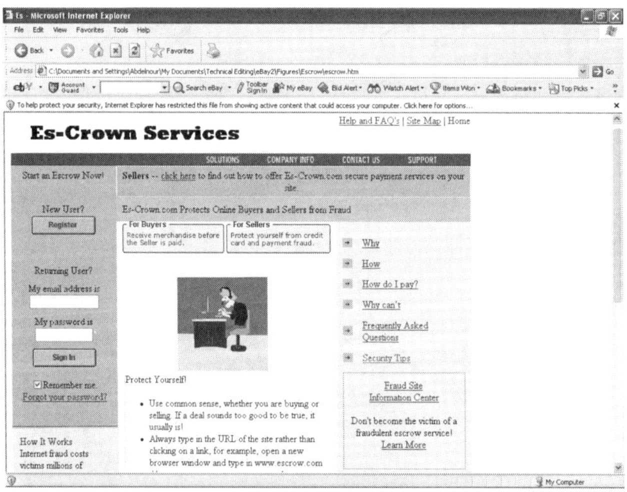

Figure 27.1 Spoof Escrow Site

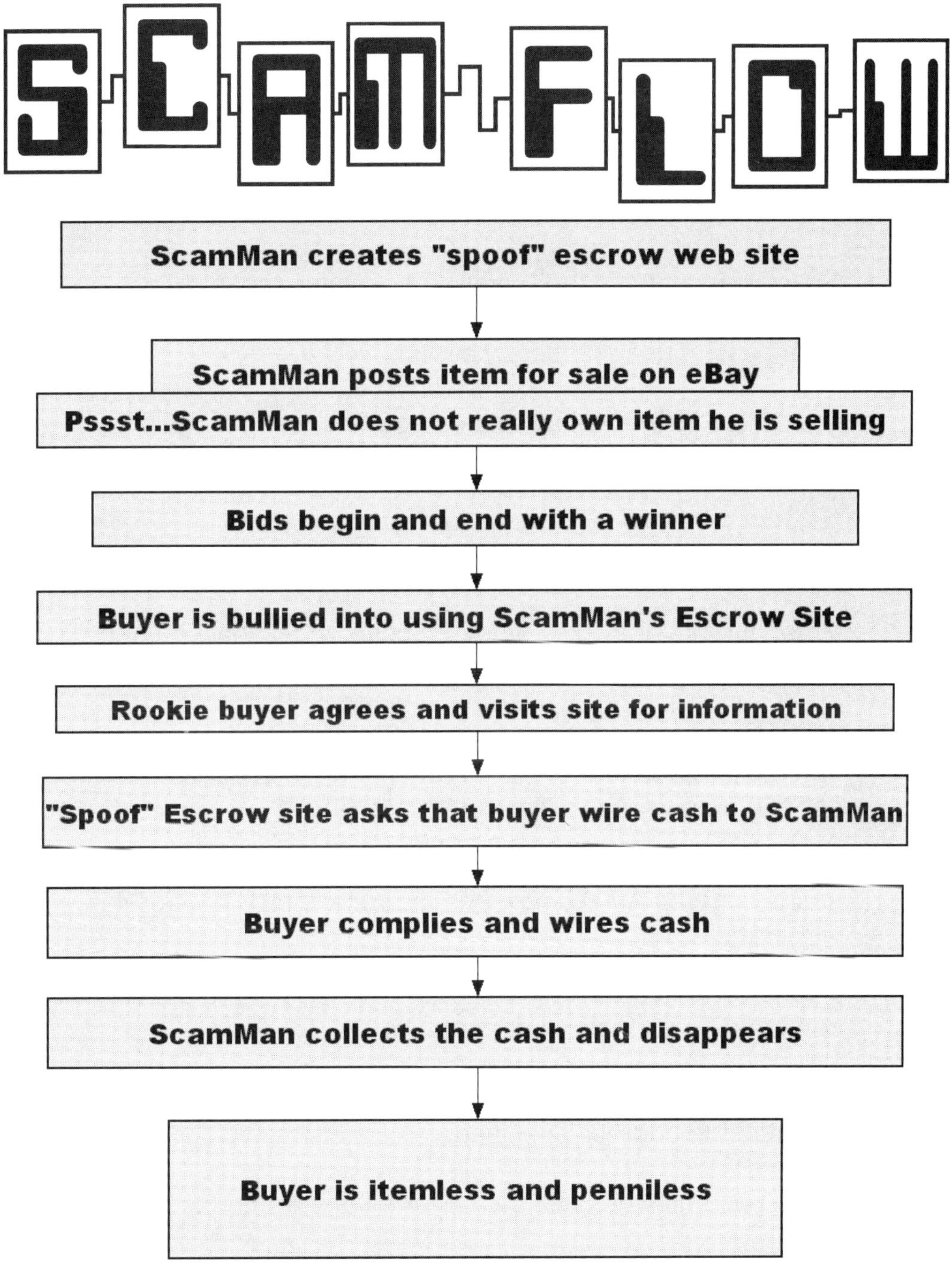
SCAM FLOW
ScamMan creates "spoof" escrow web site
ScamMan posts item for sale on eBay
Pssst...ScamMan does not really own item he is selling
Bids begin and end with a winner
Buyer is bullied into using ScamMan's Escrow Site
Rookie buyer agrees and visits site for information
"Spoof" Escrow site asks that buyer wire cash to ScamMan
Buyer complies and wires cash
ScamMan collects the cash and disappears
Buyer is itemless and penniless

2. After creating the website, ScamMan creates a listing on eBay selling a very expensive car (he doesn't have). He copies all the information from a car dealership website where there are photos and specs available.

3. Bidding begins and when the smoke clears, a victor stands atop of the pile.

4. ScamMan contacts the buyer and explains that due to previous negative experiences dealing on eBay, his preference is to use an escrow service.

5. The buyer (new to eBay and escrow services), agrees and asks for more details.

6. ScamMan points the newbie to the spoof site Es-crown.com and tells him to follow the instructions posted.

7. When the buyer arrives at the website, the following instructions and information is displayed:

- The Seller will send item to escrow organization. It will be held until Seller confirms receipt of payment. Once confirmed, Escrow organization will send item to buyer.
- Payment for item must be sent via wire transfer to seller or escrow agent. An account and address is provided for this wire transfer.
- The buyer and seller will be kept in the loop along the way via confirmation and information emails.

8. The buyer agrees to the site's terms and wires the payment to the address specified.

9. Days become weeks as the buyer awaits his item.

10. Returning to the site, he notices it no longer exists. The seller is not responding to any emails either. This buyer has been scammed – good and hard.

How does Escrow Work?

Before we continue, I think its important to explain exactly how escrow services work. Personally, I think the system is brilliant and would definitely reduce the number of scams that occur online. The following is taken from Escrow.com's website. Remember – escrow.com is eBay's preferred escrow service. For this reason, this is a trusted site to work with.

Buyer and Seller Agree to Terms

Both parties agree to terms of the transaction, which includes a description of the merchandise, sale price, number of days for the Buyer's inspection, and any shipping information.

Buyer Pays Escrow.com

The Buyer submits a payment, selecting check, money order, wire transfer, or credit card online. Escrow.com verifies the payment. Processing time varies by payment method.

Seller Ships Merchandise

Upon payment verification, the Seller is authorized to ship merchandise and submit tracking information. Escrow.com verifies that the Buyer receives the shipment.

Buyer Accepts the Merchandise

The Buyer has a set number of days for an inspection and the option to accept or reject the merchandise.

Escrow.com Pays the Seller

Escrow.com pays the Seller by check or wire transfer. The transaction is complete.

Best Defense

Now that we have a better idea of how this escrow service is supposed to work, red flags should go up when you are instructed to do something that deviates from this process.

Let's take a look at some tips and warning signs regarding escrow scams.

Listen to eBay

eBay recommends the use of only one escrow service site and that is www.escrow.com. It's never been simpler than that. There is no reason why you should use anyone else.

Escrow Bullies

Many a seller will try and bully or persuade you into using an escrow service they are "comfortable" with. Don't. The level of comfort has to be equal on both sides of the equation – not only one. Use escrow.com. Simple. Case closed.

Customer Service

If you must, and I mean must, use another escrow service, take the necessary steps to ensure they are legitimate. One way is to contact that company's customer service department and ask lots of questions. Voice mails are a dead ringer for fraud. You want to speak to a living, breathing organism and not a machine.

Email Only

Believe it or not but some of these scam sites only have email addresses where you can reach them. No good. Stay away. Run, run and did I say run? These sites are almost always spoofers. Legitimate escrow sites will have phone numbers, fax numbers, email addresses and real addresses.

Check the Domain

How long does the escrow site claim it's been in business? You can confirm by doing a "Whois" at any domain name registrar. These sites will tell you how long a domain name has been operating and who it's owned by.

Google It

Always use your preferred search engine to see if the escrow site in question comes up in the search results. You may be surprised to see it listed several times in the results – as a scam site. Try it – it will take you all of 30 seconds to do.

Spelling and Grammar

Again, we come back to poorly put together website riddled with spelling and grammatical errors. Would a real, professional escrow services site be strewn with errors? I think not. Beware.

Who Pays Whom?

When you're dealing with an escrow service, you will never be asked to send money (via wire transfer) directly to the other party in the transaction. The whole role of escrow is to act as the middle person. If wires come into play, it will be from your bank account to the escrow service's. The seller is not part of this equation.

ScamMaster I.Q. Review

Knowledge is power in the war on scammers. Here is your chance to test your scam I.Q. against the master himself; ScamMan.

Questions

1. What is an escrow?

2. True or False. The Seller sends item to escrow organization. It will be held until Seller confirms receipt of payment. Once confirmed, Escrow organization will send item to buyer.

3. True or False. Payment for item must be sent via wire transfer only to seller or escrow agent.

4. True or False. Upon payment verification, the Seller is authorized to ship merchandise and submit tracking information. Escrow.com verifies that the Buyer receives the shipment.

Answers

1. Service where third party acts as middle person for a seller and buyer

2. False. 3. False. 4. True. 5. True.

eBay Scams Presents

THE ADVENTURES OF

SCAMMAN

CHAPTER 28

Fire Sale Scam

Fire Sale Scam

Everybody loves a fire sale - lots of great items at rock bottom prices! This type of Fire Sale is a little different, especially when it's followed by the word "scam". You've heard the saying, "One man's trash is another man's treasure"? With this scam, that saying takes on a whole new meaning. Watch your back – this one can very easily slip in under the radar.

Scam Synopsis

Scammers sell absolute junk and get away with it because their listings include fallbacks like: sold as-is, not tested, returned, refurbished, etc. Buyers have no recourse due to "truths" in listing.

1. ScamMan scours his local dumps, fire sales, computer store garbage bins, neighborhood garage sales and flea markets.

2. He purchases/takes/steals computer parts and accessories that are absolute junk. They do not work and never will. If there are any valuable parts to these systems, he removes them to sell separately.

3. ScamMan then designs a very professional listing (see Figure 28.1). This listing includes several photographs of the computer/parts/accessories. From the outside, these items seem used but still in some form of working order. In all truth, they are useless pieces of junk.

SCAM FLOW

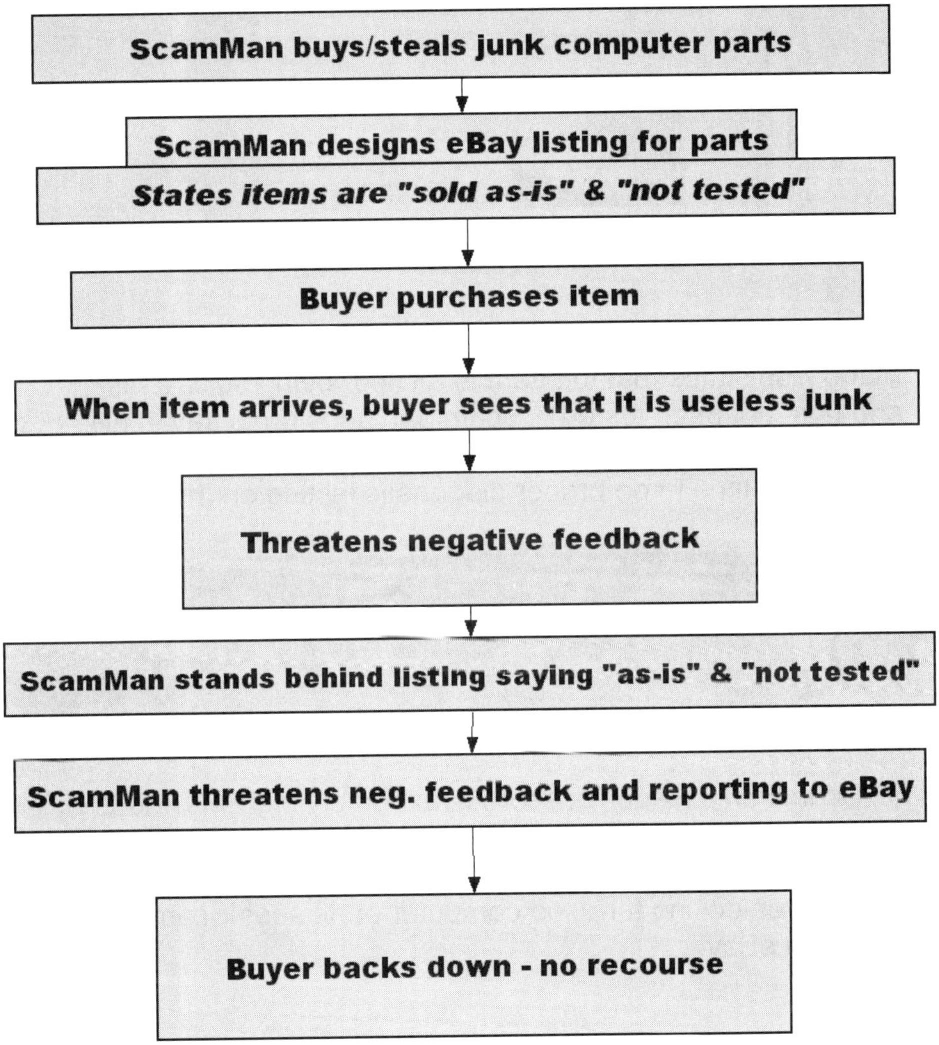
ScamMan buys/steals junk computer parts
ScamMan designs eBay listing for parts
States items are "sold as-is" & "not tested"
Buyer purchases item
When item arrives, buyer sees that it is useless junk
Threatens negative feedback
ScamMan stands behind listing saying "as-is" & "not tested"
ScamMan threatens neg. feedback and reporting to eBay
Buyer backs down - no recourse

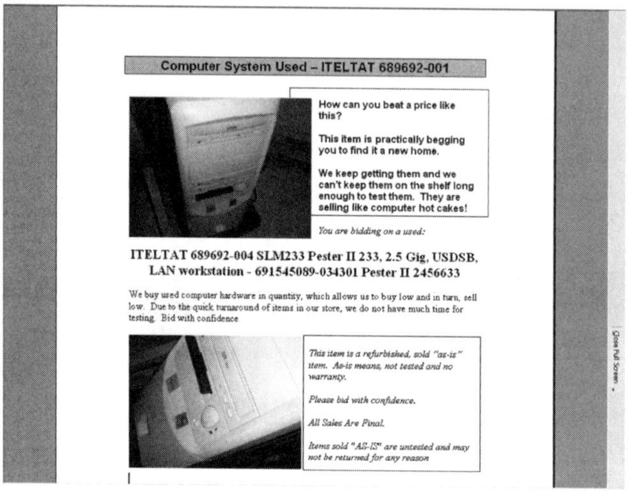

Figure 28.1 – Used Computer For Sale

4. In the listing's description, there is quite a bit of detail. The listing also states that the item is "pulled" being sold "as-is" and has "not been tested". ScamMan goes on to say in his listing that due to the high volume of sales from his "store", there is no time to do proper diagnostic testing on these items.

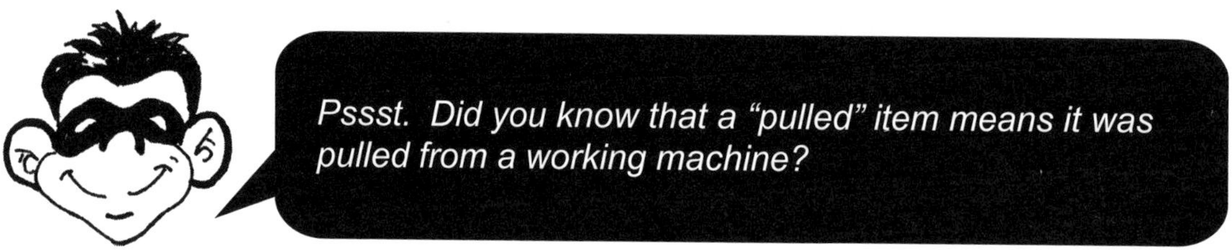

5. ScamMan's feedback score is extremely high with close to 95% positive feedback.

6. A buyer looking for used computer parts sees ScamMan's listing on eBay.

7. Intrigued, especially at the low price listed, this buyer goes for the Buy It Now option.

8. He sends his payment through to ScamMan who promptly ships out the item.

9. When the buyer receives his item, he very quickly notices that it's an absolute piece of junk with no value.

10. The buyer contacts ScamMan to complain.

11. ScamMan defends his listing by pointing to the sections that state "as-is" and "not tested".

12. The buyer threatens negative feedback if ScamMan doesn't send him a refund.

13. ScamMan returns the threat and in addition warns that he will report the buyer to eBay.

14. The buyer has absolutely no recourse due to ScamMan's deceptive word games.

Best Defense

Lots of red flags for a scam like this. The key is seeing them before it's too late. Pull out your pen and pad – the following tips are real keepers.

Item Description

How many times now have I said how important it is to read an item description extremely carefully? Two, three maybe four times now. Red flags should be going through the roof when you see the words: "sold as-is" or "not tested". These are dead giveaways to scammer on the make. Don't say you weren't warned.

Ridiculous Prices

If you see a "refurbished" hard drive for ten dollars, you have to know deep down in your heart that this is too good to be true. Always be leery of ridiculous pricing for an item you know is typically much more expensive. The deals on eBay can be really good – but can they be *that* good?

Feedback Score

Did you check that seller's feedback comments – carefully? Did you check to see exactly who is leaving all the feedback? You may notice that it's the same 2-3 people that this scammer deals with – friends perhaps? Come on – you definitely know better than that by now. Always check a seller's feedback forum. Leave no rock unturned.

Other Auctions

Make a point of checking the seller's other auctions. Do they all sound and look the same? Scammers typically run out of steam and are looking for the fast buck. In other words – they can get pretty lazy. What they'll sometimes do is include the same picture or description for all their items for sale. That's a clear sign that this cat is slippery and should be avoided at all costs.

Ask the Seller a Question

When in doubt, ask the seller a question! Ask him for more pictures or more detail regarding the item. If he's a fraud, you most likely will not get a response. At least you've saved yourself some money in the process.

ScamMaster I.Q. Review

Knowledge is power in the war on scammers. Here is your chance to test your scam I.Q. against the master himself; ScamMan.

Questions

1. What is a "pulled" item?

2. Name three different prevention strategies for the Fire Sale Scam.

3. How would you go about checking a seller's feedback comments?

4. What do you hope to gain by checking a seller's feedback comments?

5. How will checking the seller's other auctions help in avoiding becoming a victim of the fire sale scam?

Answers

1. An item taken from a working machine. 2. Read the Item Description carefully, avoid Ridiculous Prices, check Feedback Score, check the seller's other Auctions, ask the Seller a Question. 3. Click on their feedback score or on their User ID in the listing. 4. Check to see exactly who is leaving all the feedback. You may notice that it's the same 2-3 people that this scammer deals with – friends perhaps? 5. All their other listings may look exactly the same,(.e.same specs, same pix, etc.(

eBay Scams Presents

THE ADVENTURES OF

SCAMMAN

APPENDIX A

Checklists

Appendix A - Checklists

Defense Checklist for Buyers

✓	Only deal in North America.
✓	Never wire money to a seller you don't know extremely well.
✓	Be leery of any email, listing or website where spelling/grammar is an issue.
✓	Use the "Ask the Seller a Question" feature and ask questions to clarify.
✓	Check shipping & handling costs before you bid.
✓	Truly scrutinize a seller's feedback points and comments.
✓	If it's too good to be true…think twice.
✓	Read item titles and descriptions very carefully.
✓	eBay/PayPal will NEVER send you an email requesting your confidential information.
✓	If you're going to use an escrow service, only use escrow.com.
✓	Never respond to spam (not even to unsubscribe).
✓	Never deal with a seller outside of eBay's wall of protection.
✓	You will not win a car from eBay. Do not provide your confidential information.
✓	Download the eBay Toolbar (Account Guard, Report spoof sites).
✓	Report all suspicious seller activity directly to eBay.
✓	Avoid Pyramids Schemes – they don't work.
✓	Do not purchase "programs" or "systems". They don't work and are usually illegal.
✓	Always stay within the law.
✓	Use search engines like Google to research any item you are purchasing.
✓	Use bid history to check out other bidders bidding against you.
✓	Ensure that the seller's listing address is the same as the payment address.
✓	Keep a smart password and change it often.
✓	Always insure expensive items.
✓	Always request shipping vendor name, ETA and tracking number(s).

Defense Checklist for Sellers

✓	Only deal in North America.
✓	Be leery of emails from potential buyers asking obvious or stupid questions (spam).
✓	eBay/PayPal will NEVER send you an email requesting your confidential information.
✓	If you're going to use an escrow service, only use escrow.com.
✓	Never respond to spam (not even to unsubscribe).
✓	Never deal with a buyer outside of eBay's wall of protection.
✓	You will not win a car from eBay. Do not provide your confidential information.
✓	Download the eBay Toolbar (Account Guard, Report spoof sites).
✓	Report all suspicious buyer activity directly to eBay.
✓	Avoid selling/promoting Pyramids Schemes – they don't work.
✓	Do not re-sell "programs" or "systems". They don't work and are usually illegal.
✓	Always stay within the law.
✓	Use bid history to check out bidders bidding on your item (to avoid Shills).
✓	Do not accept cashier checks in amounts larger than the actual sale price.
✓	Do not sell items on behalf of another person/organization (located overseas).
✓	Feel like you're getting scammed? Use Google to see if you're not alone!
✓	Photograph/mark or record serial numbers for any item you are selling.
✓	Keep a smart password and change it often.
✓	Use services that allow you to confirm item delivery to a buyer location.

eBay Scams Presents

THE ADVENTURES OF

SCAMMAN

APPENDIX B

Scam Bites

Appendix B - Scam Bites

Here are the scams that almost got away! We didn't have the space to do a full write up but here's a quick snippet of what to watch out for!

Scam Bite#1: The Deadbeat Scam

A seller is tricked into believing a payment has been made by a scamming buyer. The seller then sends the item and later finds out he was duped.

This can be done in a variety ways:

a) After winning auction, scammer sends seller a spoof PayPal "payment notification" email. The email tells the seller that the buyer has sent payment. The seller believes the email to truly be from PayPal so he sends the item without verifying.

b) The scamming buyer steals a credit card. Sends the seller payment for the item using the stolen card. The seller sends the item to the buyer. The card is found to be stolen and all the necessary charge backs are enforced.

c) Scamming buyer pays using his credit card. Once the seller sends the item, the buyer quickly cancels his credit card with all charges claiming fraudulent use. The seller is left without funds and no item.

Scam Bite #2: Counterfeit Goods Scam

Everybody wants to keep up with Jones'. Well, in the case of eBay – the Jones' are selling a lot of their valuable goods at rock bottom prices. Everything from Gucci and Rolex watches to Tiffany jewelry and Sony Stereos, you can find them on eBay. Here's the catch: Are they real? Be careful. You could be buying into some knock-off goods.

Scam Bite #3: Hey – that's mine! Scam

Lazy scammers will outright copy a legitimate listing and sell it as their own. Once a buyer bites and purchases the item, they collect payment and disappear. If you're a legitimate seller, it's a good idea to do a check from time to time to see if someone has copied/stolen your listing. If you find someone who has, report them immediately to eBay.

Scam Bite #4: Account Buying

Like Feedback, scamming members are selling stolen eBay accounts to the highest bidders. After successfully hijacking a dormant member's account, scammers are selling these User IDs and Passwords on the black market for a lot of money. Just imagine buying an eBay account with over 1000 feedback points and 100% positive feedback! That's a lot of credibility for an eBay seller.

As an innocent buyer, these stolen accounts are obviously very difficult to detect. Use many of the tips provided (especially in the Buyer Checklist) to ensure your deal doesn't go sour.

Scam Bite #5: Pre-Approval Scam

You may sometimes come across items for sale where the seller requests that the bidder/buyer be pre-approved. This is another way of saying – call me before you bid/buy so we can talk. Upon doing so, the seller encourages the bidder/buyer to purchase the item outside of eBay's system – to save both parties money.

As you know from previous scams covered in this book, it is not recommended that you deal outside of eBay's walls. Those walls are there to protect you and if you choose to venture outside of them – you're on your own!

Index

A

B

C

D

E

F

G

H

I

J

L

M

N

O

P

Q

R

S